CULTURES OF THE WORLD®

LUXEMBOURG

Patricia Sheehan & Sakina Dhilawala

mc **Marshall Cavendish**
Benchmark
New York

PICTURE CREDITS

Cover photo: © Karl Kinne / zefa / CORBIS
alt.TYPE / Reuters: 35, 48 • Audrius Tomonis: 135 • Banque de Luxembourg: 102 • Bes Stock: 4, 6, 11, 16, 20, 50, 51, 52, 53, 62, 67, 84, 89, 94, 110, 117 • Björn Klingwall: 81, 113, 114, 115 • Bruce Yuan-Yue Bi / Lonely Planet Images: 120, 129 • Cerametal: 40 • David Simson: 3, 9, 10, 12, 38, 39, 45, 46, 57, 61, 65, 66, 68, 69, 71, 72, 74, 75, 85, 86, 90, 91, 92, 105, 108, 109, 127 • Focus Team: 15, 73, 99 • Hulton Getty: 19, 23, 24, 25, 26, 27, 78, 80 • Hutchison: 17 • Image Bank: 122 • Imedia: 13, 29, 31, 33, 41, 44, 58, 70, 87, 98, 100, 116, 118, 124, 126, 128 • International Photobank: 1, 14, 18, 64 • Leanne Logan / Lonely Planet Images: 36 • Luxembourg Ministry of Tourism: 95, 96, 97, 112, 119 • North Wind Pictures: 77 • Photolibrary / Alamy: 76, 104 • Société des Foires Internationales de Luxembourg: 42 • STOCKFOOD / Brauner, M: 130 • STOCKFOOD / Volk, Fridhelm: 131 • TOPIC: 28, 83 • Wayne Walton / Lonely Planet Images: 5, 56, 123

PRECEDING PAGE
The Grand Duchy of Luxembourg's medieval fortress, or what remains of it, juxtaposed against present-day buildings.

Publisher (U.S.): Michelle Bisson
Editors: Deborah Grahame, Mabelle Yeo
Copyreader: Daphne Hougham
Designer: Benson Tan
Cover picture researcher: Connie Gardner
Picture researcher: Thomas Khoo

Marshall Cavendish Benchmark
99 White Plains Road
Tarrytown, NY 10591
Web site: www.marshallcavendish.us

All Internet sites were correct and accurate at the time of printing. All monetary figures in this publication are in U.S. dollars.

Library of Congress Cataloging-in-Publication Data
Sheehan, Patricia, 1954–
    Luxembourg / by Patricia Sheehan & Sakina Dhilawala. — 2nd ed.
        p. cm. — (Cultures of the world)
    Summary: Discusses the geography, history, government, economy, and customs of the smallest of the Benelux countries.
        Includes bibliographical references and index.
    ISBN 978-0-7614-2088-0
    1. Luxembourg—Juvenile literature. [1. Luxembourg.] I. Dhilawala, Sakina, 1964– II. Title.
DH905.S54 2008
949.35—dc22   2007014891

Printed in China

9 8 7 6 5 4 3 2 1

CONTENTS

INTRODUCTION   5

GEOGRAPHY   7
*Green heart of Europe • Rivers and lakes • Climate
• Flora and fauna • Major cities*

HISTORY   19
*Celtic and Roman rule • A medieval world • Foreign
domination • Moves toward national independence • Wars
and occupation • Modern Luxembourg • The European Union*

GOVERNMENT   29
*Constitutional rights • Representation of the people
• Public administration • Local government • Law of the land
• The royal family • The political divide • Women in politics*

ECONOMY   37
*A success story • Workforce • Social consensus • An eye for
opportunities • Industry • Trade fairs • Financial services
• Agriculture • Tourism • Exports and imports • Energy*

ENVIRONMENT   49
*Climate change • Waste management • Biodiversity • Land and
water habitat • Protecting the environment*

LUXEMBOURGERS   57
*Population trends • National pride • Character and personality
• Melting pot • Dress • Prominent Luxembourgers*

LIFESTYLE   65
*Standard of living • Hearth and home • Family values
• Women • Young people • Education • The welfare state
• Crime and punishment • Green living*

Castle ruins near the town of Diekirch offer a reminder of Luxembourg's rich medieval past.

3

RELIGION   **77**
*From Druidism to Christianity • A medieval center
• The Protestant challenge • Witchcraft • Religion today
• Places of worship*

LANGUAGE   **85**
*Rivalry of languages • Three languages, three uses
• Luxembourgish in the arts • Standardizing Luxembourgish
• Learning Luxembourgish • Popular names • Broadcasting
and newspapers*

ARTS   **95**
*Archaeology • Traditional crafts • Theater and cinema
• Music • Painting and sculpture • Cultural monuments
and architecture • Modern architecture*

LEISURE   **105**
Vacations • National sports • Recreation • Entertainment

FESTIVALS   **111**
*National Day • Easter • Christmas • New Year • Customs and
rituals • Fairs and fetes • Religious festivals*

FOOD   **121**
*Traditional fare • Eating habits • Specialties • A nation
of drinkers • Wines • Seasonal foods • Eating out*

MAP OF LUXEMBOURG   **132**

ABOUT THE ECONOMY   **135**

ABOUT THE CULTURE   **137**

TIME LINE   **138**

GLOSSARY   **140**

FURTHER INFORMATION   **141**

BIBLIOGRAPHY   **142**

INDEX   **142**

The guarded grand ducal palace in the heart of Luxembourg City.

INTRODUCTION

THE GRAND DUCHY OF LUXEMBOURG is a small country, landlocked by Belgium, France, and Germany, and its history has been infamously linked with those of its far larger neighbors. Nonetheless, Luxembourg has managed to carve out its place as an independent nation with its own unique culture. It is among the richest nations in Western Europe, with a thriving banking and financial industry and successes on other economic fronts.

Luxembourg became a founding member of a customs union—a common trade agreement—with Belgium and the Netherlands in 1944 and of the European Economic Community, a forerunner of the European Union, in 1957. Approximately one-third of Luxembourg's population are foreigners. With so many different nationalities working and living within its borders, Luxembourg has become one of the Continent's most cosmopolitan countries.

GEOGRAPHY

LUXEMBOURG IS ONE OF the nations, along with Belgium and the Netherlands, collectively known as the Benelux countries. This name arose from the trading partnerships established after World War II.

Luxembourg is smaller than the state of Rhode Island. It measures 55 miles (89 km) long and 35 miles (56 km) wide, covering some 998 square miles (2,585 square km). Triangular in shape—bordering Belgium in the north and west, Germany in the east, and France in the south—with 221 miles (356 km) of borders, the country is completely landlocked.

Despite its small size, Luxembourg has a varied topography, with two main features in the landscape. The northern section of the country is formed by part of the plateau of the Ardennes, where the mountains range from 1,293 to almost 1,837 feet (394–560 m) high. The rest of the country is made up of undulating countryside with broad valleys. The capital, Luxembourg City, is located in this southern part of the country.

GREEN HEART OF EUROPE

The most prominent landmark, the high plateau of the Ardennes in the north, took nature millions of years to carve. At its highest point, it reaches a height of 1,837 feet (560 m). Commonly known as the Oesling, the Ardennes region covers 320 square miles (828 square km), about 32 percent of the entire country.

Rugged scenery predominates in the Ardennes because river erosion over thousands of years has left a varied, low-mountain landscape, densely covered with vegetation, sometimes with considerable variations in height. These differences in relief, together with stretches of water interspersed with forests, fields, and pastures, are the main features that make the landscape so distinctive. Typical of this high area, however,

Opposite: **Oak and beech trees are found in Luxembourg's forests, which cover a vast expanse of the country's terrain.**

The main principle underlying ecosystem protection in the Upper Sûre Natural Park is that the environment is an integrated network in which each element interacts and affects the functioning of the whole.

is infertile soil and poor drainage, resulting in numerous peat bogs that were once excavated for fuel. These factors, combined with heavy rainfall and frost, made this an inhospitable environment for the first settlers.

Even today, the living conditions in such an environment are not particularly inviting. Nevertheless, some 7,800 people make their living off the land, either through forestry, small-scale farming, or environmental work. Because the soil is so difficult to cultivate, most of the land is used for cattle pasture. The Ardennes region also includes the Upper Sûre Natural Park, an important conservation area and a hikers' retreat.

South of the Sûre River the country is known as the Gutland, meaning "Good Land." This region covers slightly over two-thirds of the country. The terrain gently rises and falls with an average elevation of

THE UPPER SÛRE NATURAL PARK

Located in the far northwest of the Oesling region, the natural park is primarily an area of conservation with a specially protected zone for wild birds. The objectives of the park are threefold.

First, and most importantly, the aim is to protect the natural environment and ecosystem. This means conserving the indigenous flora and fauna as well as protecting the purity of air and water and monitoring soil quality. A second goal is to develop economic activity, mostly forestry and low-density tourism, as a means of creating employment and a high quality of life. As a result, the transportation infrastructure in the park is excellent. The third objective is to preserve the architectural heritage of the area, which ranges from large numbers of chapels and abandoned mills to former slate quarries and castle ruins.

For visitors to the park, there is a host of leisure activities, from nature walks to tours of cultural monuments to water sports on Upper Sûre Lake. More than 310 miles (500 km) of well-maintained footpaths make this a popular spot for day-trippers, as well as providing a large choice of accommodations for vacationers. A fair and festival is held in the park annually on the first weekend in July.

700 feet (213 m). River erosion in this area has created deep gorges and caves, resulting in some spectacular scenery.

Agriculture is the main activity, as the word "Gutland" refers to its fertile soils and the warm, dry summers experienced in this part of the duchy compared with the Oesling region.

As a result, vegetables and such fruits as strawberries, apples, plums, and cherries are grown in large quantities.

In the extreme south of the country lies "the land of the red rocks," a reference to the deposits of minerals found there. Rich in iron ore—sought after and exploited from Roman, if not earlier, times—the area is a mining and heavy-industry region that stretches for over 12.4 miles (20 km). The tall chimneys of the iron and steel works are typical landmarks of the industrial south.

To the east lies the grape-growing valley of the Moselle River. Numerous villages nestle in the deep valleys and behind the vineyards along the riverbanks. Every village has at least one winery. Also in the east, around the town of Echternach, is the "Little Switzerland" area, characterized by wooded glens and ravines with unusual rock formations.

Beef cattle are raised on the plentiful green pastures of the hill slopes near Vianden in the northeastern part of Luxembourg.

Luxembourg City is sometimes thought of as the center of Western Europe. It is 223 miles (359 km) from Amsterdam, 206 miles (332 km) from Paris, and 246 miles (396 km) from Zurich.

9

Luxembourg's vineyards produce wines that are especially appreciated in Belgium, with some 80 percent of exports going to that neighbor.

RIVERS AND LAKES

Luxembourg has a number of minor rivers, such as the Eisch, the Alzette, and the Pétrusse, but the main river is the Moselle with its tributaries—the Sûre and the Our. Together, their courses serve as a natural boundary between Luxembourg and Germany. Many of Luxembourg's medieval castles can be found along their banks.

The Moselle River actually rises in eastern France and flows north through Luxembourg for 23 miles (37 km) to join the mighty Rhine River at Koblenz, Germany. The Moselle is 339 miles (545 km) long, and is navigable, because of canalization, for more than 40 miles (64 km). Green slopes covered with grapevines flank the meandering course of the river.

Rising in Belgium, the Sûre River flows for 107 miles (172 km) in an easterly direction through Luxembourg and into the Moselle. Its sinuous course essentially cuts Luxembourg from east to west. The Our River flows along the northeastern border and joins the Sûre after 31 miles (50 km). Its valley is surrounded by unspoiled countryside.

The Upper Sûre lake is the largest stretch of water in the grand duchy. Ringed with luxuriant vegetation and peaceful creeks, the lake is a center for such water sports as sailing, canoeing, and kayaking. The many outdoor activities, which make it an attractive spot for visitors, have led to the growth of a local crafts industry.

The town of Esch-sur-Sûre sits at one end of the lake. Immediately above it the river has been dammed to form a hydroelectric reservoir extending some 6 miles (10 km) up the valley. The Upper Sûre dam was built in the sixties to meet the country's drinking water requirements.

The Moselle River, which has its source in the Vosges Mountains of France, eventually flows into the Rhine in Germany. On the left of the photo is a view of vineyards near Nittel near Trier in Germany, and Machtum, near Grevenmacher in the Grand Duchy of Luxembourg, can be seen on the right.

CLIMATE

Luxembourg is part of the West European Continental climatic region and so enjoys a temperate climate without great extremes. Winters are mild, summers fairly cool, and rainfall is high.

The northern and southern regions, however, have somewhat different seasonal weathers. In the north there is considerable influence from the Atlantic systems, in which the passage of frequent pressure depressions gives rise to unstable weather conditions. This results in changeable weather with constant overcast skies and considerable drizzle in the winter.

Luxembourg's rainfall reaches 49 inches (125 cm) a year in some areas. In the summer, excessive heat is rare and temperature levels drop noticeably at night. Luxembourg's low temperatures and humidity make for what those living in the northern part of the country call, optimistically, an "invigorating climate."

In the south, although the rainfall is not significantly lower, at around 32 inches (80 cm), and the winters are no milder, the principal difference is in the higher summer temperatures, especially in the Moselle valley. Crops, especially wine grapes, thrive there. With a mean annual temperature of 50°F (10°C), the

THE OTTER

The otter has a slender body, weighing 13–33 pounds (6–15 kg), with a long neck, small ears, and short legs. The base of its tail is almost as thick as its body. With its webbed feet, it is an accomplished swimmer and can travel underwater for a quarter of a mile (0.4 km) without surfacing for air. Even on land, the otter can move faster than a human can run.

It eats small aquatic animals like fish and frogs, and also preys on small mammals and birds. A playful animal, an otter's favorite pastime is sliding down steep banks of mud or snow and plunging into water or snowdrifts.

sunniest months are May to August. In spring, the countryside is a riot of bright wildflowers and fragrant fruit blossoms.

FLORA AND FAUNA

Luxembourg's flora is determined by the country's location at the border between the Atlantic-European and Central European vegetation zones. In the north, beech and oak trees are plentiful. The oak trees can grow to 100–150 feet (30–45 m) high, with diameters of 4–8 feet (1.2–2.4 m). They yield large quantities of excellent hardwood lumber highly prized for its strength, durability, and beauty.

Above: **A field of red poppies in full bloom in the countryside.**

Opposite: **Wine experts believe it is the spring and summer weather that determines the quality of wine that is produced in Luxembourg.**

Along the riverbanks, species like black alder and willow can be found. Alder wood is pale yellow to reddish brown, fine-textured, and durable even under water. It is often used in furniture and guitar making. It is also an important timber tree, mainly because of its disease-resistant properties. Willow trees can reach a height of 65 feet (20 m) and are valued for ornamental landscaping purposes and for basket weaving.

The narrow, deeply incised valleys of the north also provide a habitat for rare plants and animals, especially the otter, a protected species. In the industrial south, among the abandoned quarries and deserted open-pit mines, nature has reclaimed her own and flowers bloom everywhere.

An aerial view of a part of Luxembourg City, the multicultural capital.

MAJOR CITIES

With Luxembourg's small population, the only true city is the capital itself. The typical settlement in Luxembourg is a small town, with most people choosing this type of community rather than residing in the countryside.

LUXEMBOURG CITY The capital occupies a dramatic and picturesque site on a high point above precipitous cliffs that drop to the narrow valleys of the Alzette and Pétrusse rivers. The 230-foot (70-m) deep gorge cut by the Alzette, spanned by bridges and viaducts, adds to the charm of the city. Although the original fortress over which Luxembourg City is built was demolished in 1867, some of the defensive fortifications remain intact. These provide superb viewpoints across the city, and they offer an opportunity to visit the casemates, which used to hold cannon, hewn into the rock.

Despite progressive urbanization, the capital still retains a certain tranquillity. There are numerous shops selling international goods, bistros, and restaurants with intriguing specialties from all over the world. The combination of multilingual cultural events, its central location, space for offices and businesses, as well as excellent transportation links, make Luxembourg a capital city of renown in Europe. At the last census, in 2001, it had a population of 76,688.

ESCH-SUR-ALZETTE This is the second largest urban area in the country and the principal one in the industrial south. Located near the French border, the town is an ancient settlement that can be traced back more than 5,000 years. Its name is derived from the Celtic word *esk*, meaning a stream. Esch-sur-Alzette has an acknowledged reputation both as a business center and as an architectural town, because of its art deco houses.

Luxembourg City is a cosmopolitan European capital with much in the way of evening entertainment, especially in the warmer months.

The cosmopolitan town, with a large number of foreign residents, also has numerous forms of entertainment and cultural attractions. At Rumelange, about 4 miles (6 km) outside the town, is a museum featuring mining memorabilia of the 19th and 20th centuries. The site of a famous grotto of Our Lady in Kayl, with the purported healing properties of the waters of the spring, is very close to the town. Some 27,000 people live in Esch-sur-Alzette.

A view of Luxembourg City and a part of the Alzette River.

DUDELANGE, **DIFFERDANGE**, and **BELVAUX**, with populations of 17,320, 10,248, and 5,113 respectively, are all industrial towns with economies based on the iron and steel industries. They each have commercial centers, with pleasant parks and recreational sites.

ECHTERNACH This town lies on the banks of the Sûre, which forms the border with Germany. The town of 4,610 residents is especially well known for the dancing procession that takes place each Whit Tuesday, some weeks after Easter. The old patrician houses, narrow streets, seventh-century Benedictine abbey, and ancient walls have helped Echternach to retain a remarkable medieval atmosphere.

The town square in Echternach. The town was once one of the most important religious centers of Europe. It was here that the art of medieval manuscript illumination developed and reached its height during the 11th century.

HISTORY

THE RICH HISTORY OF LUXEMBOURG explains how one of the smallest independent states in the world came into existence and how a population no greater than that of an average European city has developed an unmistakable culture, language, and identity.

Luxembourg was once a larger country, owning large areas of what are now Belgium, France, and Germany, but foreign domination has over time reduced the territory of Luxembourg considerably.

CELTIC AND ROMAN RULE

The Celts, early inhabitants of Luxembourg, were an Iron Age people, able to make more sophisticated weapons than their predecessors, who used only stone and bone for tools. They were a strong race of warriors who drove chariots and confronted one another in single combat. But despite their strength and resistance, they were no competition for Julius Caesar, who arrived in Western Europe in 58 B.C. and conquered all the land up to the Rhine River.

By 15 B.C., Luxembourg, along with the other two Low Countries, Belgium and the Netherlands, had become an imperial province of the Roman Empire under Emperor Augustus. Roman rule continued until the middle of the fifth century, when the Germanic Franks overran most of the country. By the eighth century, the Frankish king, Charlemagne, had been declared emperor by the pope.

For the next 200 years, until the 10th century, the former imperial province was the object of continuous fighting by rival counts, lords, and dukes.

Above: **Julius Caesar overran Gaul and the surrounding region, including Luxembourg, in a series of military campaigns between 58 and 50 B.C.**

Opposite: **This architecture is a reminder of the grand duchy's medieval past.**

Vianden Castle, one of the many medieval forts found around the country.

Before the 14th century, there had been little outside interest in the Low Countries, but when thriving fishing, shipping, and textile industries developed, foreign rulers were quick to move in.

A MEDIEVAL WORLD

Between the 10th and 14th centuries, the County of Luxembourg began to take shape. A tower had been built many years earlier on an important crossroad, forming part of the Roman defense system against Germanic tribes. Known as the Castellum Lucilinburhuc (CA-stel-um LUK-in-burr-huk), or "Little Castle," this stronghold became the property of Siegfried, Count of the Ardennes, in 963.

He immediately began to build a fortified castle on a neighboring rock known as the "Bock," at the junction of two rivers, the Alzette and the Pétrusse. This castle became the foundation of the city of Luxembourg and, over the course of time, strong circular walls were built for its defense.

Luxembourg was able to remain independent until the 14th century mainly because of several strong personalities who emerged during this period. One of the most important was Countess Ermesinda (1186–1247), in the 13th century, who ruled for over 20 years. During her reign, Ermesinda extended the frontiers of Luxembourg substantially, not by war but through the peaceful means of marriage alliances. In those times, marriages were more powerful than wars in terms of allegiance and loyalty.

Another powerful figure was the 14th-century Count John the Blind (1296–1346). By the age of 41, he had completely lost his sight. Nonetheless, he managed to increase Luxembourg's holdings, stimulate the economy, set up a new defense system, and build new fortifications. John personified the medieval knight for whom honor, loyalty, and courage were key values. He remains a national hero to Luxembourgers today.

ERMESINDA—THE FOUNDING LADY OF LUXEMBOURG

Ermesinda, born as the only heir when her father was 40 years old, was betrothed from birth to one of the most powerful princes in the Kingdom of France, the count of Champagne. The count, however, married the queen of Jerusalem instead, and so Ermesinda, at the tender age of 12, was "passed" to a cousin of hers, Count Theobald. During the life of Theobald, then already in his forties and a grandfather from a first marriage, Ermesinda took little part in political affairs.

On Theobold's death in 1214, she was a young widow of 27 and a desirable match, with four daughters but no male heir. At the beginning of the 13th century, succession through the female line was not ensured, and so to protect her inheritance she married a German prince with whom she had a son, Henry V.

Upon the death of her second husband, in 1226, Ermesinda began a personal reign that lasted 20 years—a considerable length of rule in medieval times—until her son came of age. During this period, she established the foundations of the Luxembourgian state, granted a charter to the City of Luxembourg, and proved to be a political woman of great maturity. Under her rule, the citizens of Luxembourg gained much personal freedom, including the right to sell possessions, organize themselves, and create institutions. Ermesinda is remembered as the founder of Luxembourg.

Under the rule of his son Charles IV (1316–78), Luxembourg reached its greatest expanse, through treaties and his own and family marriages. In 1354 Luxembourg's status was raised from that of a county of the Holy Roman Empire to a duchy by Charles IV. The duchy of Luxembourg was formed by integrating the old county of Luxembourg, the marquisat of Arlon, the counties of Durbuy, Vianden, and Laroche, and the districts of Thionville, Bitburg, and Marville to form a single political entity.

FOREIGN DOMINATION

From the 15th to the 18th centuries Luxembourg and the other Low Countries fell under a succession of foreign rulers—the French Burgundians, the Austrian Habsburgs, the Spanish, and then the French again. By 1506, with the king of Spain in power, the Netherlands had become disillusioned with both Catholicism and Spanish rule. The Dutch rebelled in 1566 and declared their independence. Luxembourg and Belgium remained Catholic and under Spanish control, with a brief return to Austrian rule, until the invasion by French Revolutionary troops in 1795. Through annexation, much of Luxembourg's territory became part of France.

At the peak of its political power in the 14th and 15th centuries, Luxembourg provided four rulers who served as Holy Roman emperors. The Holy Roman Empire consisted of lands from western and central Europe ruled over by Frankish and then German kings for 10 centuries.

LUXEMBOURG'S HISTORY TILL THE 19TH CENTURY

A.D. 658	Saint Wilibrord of Utrecht, Bishop of Utrecht, Apostle of the Frisians, and son of Saint Hilgis born; dies at Echternach, Luxembourg, 739.
A.D. 843	Treaty of Verdun partitions Charlemagne's empire among the three sons of Louis I.
1506	Luxembourg goes over to the Habsburg dynasty of Spain when Charles V inherits Burgundian possessions from his father and Spanish possessions from his mother.
1659	Following the Treaty of the Pyrenees, Spain yields the southern part of Luxembourg (Thionville and dependencies) to Louis XIV.
1713–14	After the Spanish Civil War, the treaties of Utrecht and Rastadt share the Spanish heritage. Charles VI of Habsburg receives Luxembourg, which thus becomes Austrian property.
1795	After the French Revolution, French troops besiege the fortress of Luxembourg, which capitulates after six months.
1815	After the defeat of Napoleon, territories acquired under his authority are restored. Luxembourg is elevated to the rank of a grand duchy and becomes a sovereign state. William I of Orange-Nassau becomes grand duke of Luxembourg and king of the Netherlands.
1839	The Treaty of London is signed (after the Belgian Revolution, in 1830); the Great Powers confirm the status of independence of the grand duchy. Nevertheless, Luxembourg is divided into two parts, the western part going to Belgium and the eastern part continuing to form the sovereign grand duchy. The country takes on its definite geographical form.
1866	Dissolution of the Germanic Confederation, which Luxembourg had belonged to since 1815.
1867	Napoleon III proposes the purchase of Luxembourg from Grand Duke William III. Bismarck opposes this idea. The "question of Luxembourg" is resolved by the signature of the Treaty of London, which grants Luxembourg the status of a "perpetually neutral and disarmed" state.
1890	After the death of Grand Duke William III, who died without a male heir, the grand ducal succession passes to Adolphe of Nassau-Weilburg (1817–1905).

Opposite: **In the 1815 Congress of Vienna, the European powers feared leaving Luxembourg, with its strategic position and fortifications, prey to invaders, and made the Dutch king, William I, and his heirs the hereditary grand dukes of Luxembourg.**

MOVES TOWARD NATIONAL INDEPENDENCE

The modern Luxembourg state has its origins in the Treaty of Vienna in 1815, which attempted to reorganize Europe after the defeat of Napoleon Bonaparte. The duchy was raised to the rank of a grand duchy and became part of the Kingdom of the Netherlands, along with the Netherlands and Belgium.

GIBRALTAR OF THE NORTH

Over a period of 400 years, the fortress of Luxembourg was besieged, devastated, and rebuilt more than 20 times. In 1795 the French general Lazare Carnot described the city as "second only to Gibraltar," a reference to the famous Rock of Gibraltar at the southern tip of Spain, which also was repeatedly attacked but rarely captured. Praise indeed for the impregnability of Luxembourg's fortress.

Under the international Treaty of London, in 1867, which granted independence to Luxembourg, it was agreed that the old fortress, considered a symbol of war and devastation, needed to be destroyed. By then, after nine centuries of military construction, the fortress had, for its defense, three battlements: the first battlement was fortified with bastions, the second included 15 forts, and the third was composed of an exterior wall containing nine forts. The fortress had, in addition, 47,840 square yards (40,000 square m) of military barracks. The dismantling took 16 years to complete, although some of it was spared.

Thus it is possible today to walk inside the imposing remains of one of the most powerful fortresses in Europe. Some 7 miles (11 km) of the former 15 miles (24 km) of underground defenses called casemates (basically tunnels cut deep into the rock to give besieged troops shelter and room for workshops and kitchens) still exist. It was impossible to destroy the casemates without also destroying the city, so only the main connections and entrances were closed. Some of the casemates have several floors connected by huge staircases descending more than 120 feet (36.6 m). Used as bomb shelters during World War II, they also doubled as nuclear shelters during the Cold War.

By 1839 Belgium had established itself as an independent kingdom, and Luxembourg was subsequently partitioned, losing much of its territory to the new Belgian state. Not until 1867 in the Treaty of London was Luxembourg, greatly reduced in size, formally recognized as independent and guaranteed permanent neutrality.

A union with the Netherlands ended in 1890 when King William III of the Netherlands died and Wilhelmina became queen. Luxembourg would not recognize Wilhelmina as monarch because there lived a male heir, Duke Adolphe, in a branch of the House of Luxembourg, so he became the grand duke of Luxembourg.

WARS AND OCCUPATION

During World War I, despite its neutrality, Luxembourg was occupied by German troops. After the war ended, Luxembourg severed all previous economic ties with Germany, and the grand duchy joined Belgium in an economic union in 1921. Until the outbreak of World War II, the grand duchy, under the reign of Grand Duchess Charlotte, made good economic progress.

In May 1940, German troops invaded Luxembourg and the duchess was forced to flee. She established a government in exile in England. Thousands of young men were pressed into German armies by the Nazi occupiers, although a strong Resistance movement was organized. After five years of occupation, Allied forces under American general George S. Patton's command finally liberated Luxembourg in April 1945.

MODERN LUXEMBOURG

Grand Duchess Charlotte reigned for 45 years, from 1919 to 1964, a period of general prosperity for Luxembourgers, except for the interruptions of World War II. Grand Duke Jean (born 1921) succeeded to the throne after the abdication of his mother in 1964. He reigned until 2000, when his son Henri (born 1955) became grand duke. Henri is married to Maria Teresa Mestre (born in Havana, Cuba, 1956).

In 1948, after the deprivations of World War II, Luxembourg gave up its neutrality by joining various international organizations. These included the United Nations (UN), the North Atlantic Treaty Organization (NATO), and the Organization for Economic Cooperation and Development (OECD).

An early portrait of Grand Duchess Charlotte. She died in 1985.

William II (ruled 1840–49) is arguably the duchy's most respected Dutch ruler.

24

BATTLE OF THE BULGE

With Allied successes escalating on all fronts, it appeared that Germany would be defeated by Christmas 1944. But attention focused sharply on Luxembourg that December 16, when it became clear that the Germans had started a major offensive through the northern part of its captive territory, which American troops had already liberated on September 10, 1944.

General George Patton had envisioned a German surprise attack and, as a result, had three contingency plans drawn up. He transmitted one of these to his army, and the entire force made a 90-degree turn toward the north, pushing through Luxembourg. They hit the advancing German units in the flanks on the southern shoulder of the "bulge," or salient—a military term used to describe the bulge in the Allies' line that the Germans had caused by their advance. During fierce combat, with many casualties, that took place under adverse winter conditions, Patton's army finally defeated the enemy by the end of January. The Battle of the Bulge exhausted Nazi Germany's last operational reserves, and, by May 1945, they had unconditionally surrendered.

Despite this resounding success, Patton was relieved of his command in October 1945 because of the general's fierce antagonism toward communism. In addition, convinced that his destiny lay in military glory, Patton was known for his arrogance and vanity, which, unfortunately, earned him many enemies. Others, however, saw him as a true Southern gentleman, prizing bravery above all other virtues. Nevertheless, he remains a national hero to Luxembourgers. In December 1945, Patton died as a result of an automobile accident and is buried in the Hamm U.S. military cemetery in Luxembourg, at the head of the fallen soldiers from the Third Army he had commanded.

Through these organizations, and the Benelux Customs Union in 1948 with Belgium and the Netherlands, Luxembourg has supported a policy of cooperation on the international front and, in the post-war period, has enjoyed unprecedented peace and economic prosperity.

In 1951 Luxembourg and the two other Benelux countries, plus Germany, France, and Italy, decided to form the six-member European Coal and Steel Community (ECSC). Playing a major role in this plan was Foreign Minister Robert Schuman of France, who was Luxembourg-born and raised.

Grand Duke Jean and Princess Josephine-Charlotte after their marriage ceremony in 1953.

Based on the understanding that if an individual nation does not alone control its armaments and heavy industries, then it can no longer declare war, the ECSC became the first step toward European integration.

THE EUROPEAN UNION

The second stage of European unification came soon after, in 1958, with the establishment of the European Economic Community (EEC), an institution set up to facilitate free trade of goods and services among the six member countries. By 1990, membership had increased to 12. The Maastricht Treaty, the third stage, led to the creation of the European Union (EU) in 1993 that set the stage for the even more ambitious goal of future political and monetary solidarity.

As of January 2007, there were 27 member nations of the EU, all with market economies and with a combined population of some 420 million people. Free movement of goods and capital now makes it possible to trade and invest money anywhere in the Union. And free movement of people means that citizens of any EU country can travel, reside, study, and work wherever they wish in the Union.

There are also common agreements on foreign, security, and agricultural policies, as well as on justice and domestic affairs issues. An important landmark of the EU was its achieving the goal of monetary union.

The idea of a single currency was first introduced at the Hague Summit in 1969. Because of the unfavorable worldwide economic climate then, it could not be applied. The idea was nevertheless relaunched, and the euro came into being—in theory, at first—in January 1999. Three years later, in January 2002, euro notes and coins were introduced and put into circulation in the participating countries.

By 2006, 13 member nations of the EU had adopted the euro as their common currency. Those countries, frequently referred to as the Eurozone, include Austria, Belgium, Finland, France, Germany, Ireland, Italy, Luxembourg, the Netherlands, Portugal, Spain, Slovenia, and Greece.

At European Union meetings, the Council of Ministers has a mandate to reach compromises, without any single government's being placed at a disadvantage. Proposals for laws are presented to this Council, after being drawn up by the European Commission. Every member has a full veto power. This means that, in some circumstances, Luxembourg, or any other member nation, can veto legislation that all the other member states have supported.

The Commission is led by a president who is chosen by the European Council with the approval of the European Parliament. Jacques Santer, a former prime minister of Luxembourg, served as president of the European Commission from 1995 to 1999. Though a European Parliament plays a steadily increasing role in the drafting of EU laws, it does not yet have the power equivalent to national parliaments. The Court of Justice ensures that EU law is carried out.

Today Luxembourg is a major supporter and force behind European economic and political unification. Both the government and the people take the issue seriously and understand that there can be no future outside a European Union for such a small country as Luxembourg.

The European Union of today began with a plan proposed by Frenchman Jean Monnet in 1950 to Robert Schuman (*above*). Luxembourg-born Schuman took up the initiative enthusiastically and pushed hard for the creation of the European Coal and Steel Community a year later.

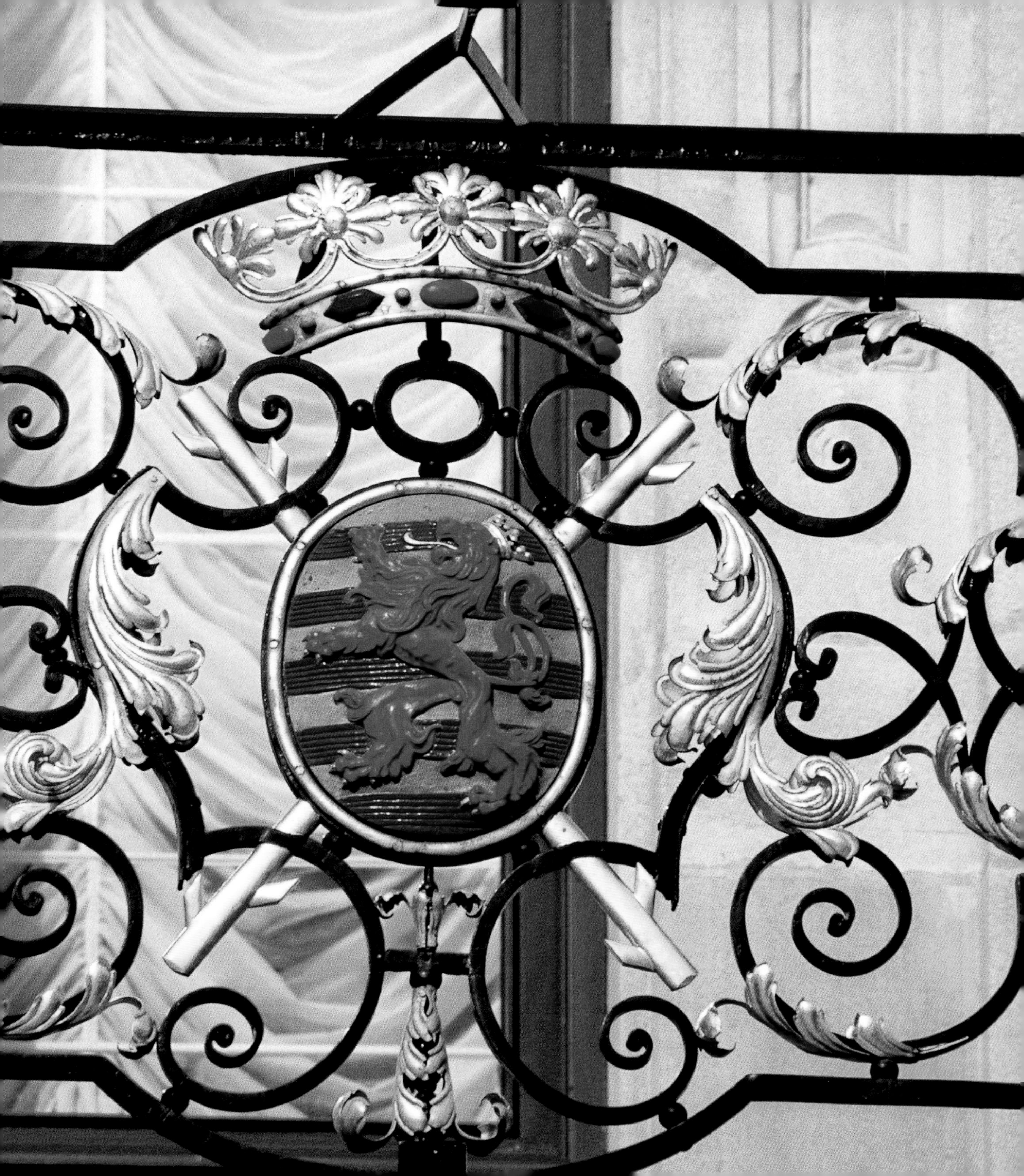

GOVERNMENT

THE STATE OF LUXEMBOURG is a constitutional monarchy. Ultimate power resides with the people through their elected representatives, although there is a hereditary monarch in the country. Under Luxembourg's constitution, the grand duke or grand duchess and the cabinet exercise executive power.

If a need arises to consult the people directly on a particular issue of national importance, a referendum can be called. Results of such a referendum, however, are not binding on the government.

CONSTITUTIONAL RIGHTS

In the first few decades of its independence, Luxembourg lived through four different constitutions. The current one was adopted in 1868 and has been amended several times—the last in 1998—to make the constitution more democratic. One of the most important amendments was the restriction of the monarch's power in the making of laws.

Article 36 of the constitution now bars the grand duke from suspending laws or from dispensing with their enforcement. In theory, he sanctions the laws and still could veto anything passed by the Chamber of Deputies, but this right of veto has not been used since 1919 and is unlikely to be tolerated in a democratic country.

The constitution guarantees the rights of citizens and regulates the organization of public authorities. Equality before the law, individual freedom, freedom of opinion and the press, freedom of worship, the right to state education, and the right to work are some of the public rights specified by the constitution.

Above: **Voting is compulsory in Luxembourg's elections. Abstention without justification incurs a fine that increases each time the offense is repeated.**

Opposite: **Luxembourg's state emblem.**

REPRESENTATION OF THE PEOPLE

For the purpose of the general elections, the country is divided into four electoral districts. Sixty deputies have been elected every five years by universal suffrage since 1919. Elections of these deputies are based on proportional representation among the various political parties.

According to the Luxembourg constitution, legislative power belongs jointly to the grand duke and this 60-member Chamber of Deputies. Legislation is introduced to the Chamber by the grand duke, who exercises executive power together with the cabinet—including the prime minister and other ministers—and in accordance with the constitution of 1868. When a bill has passed through, it goes to the grand duke for approval. The grand duke has the power to dissolve or replace the legislature.

There is also a 21-member advisory body called the Council of State, with members being appointed for life by the grand duke. This Council of State is not a democratically elected institution and decisions made by it can be overturned. The extent of its power is to delay and examine laws, not to prevent them. Nevertheless, members are required to discuss bills, and no final vote can be taken on any bill by the Chamber before the Council's opinion has been heard.

Executive power is exercised by the Council of Ministers, presently 11 ministers and two state secretaries, and is led by the prime minister, who is the head of the political party with the most parliamentary seats. The prime minister selects ministers, taking care to ensure the shaping of a cabinet that has the support of the majority of the Chamber. Ministers are then officially appointed by the grand duke. Each minister is responsible for a particular branch of public administration. They can speak in the Chamber of Deputies, but they are not members of it. In 2007 the prime minister was Jean-Claude Juncker, who was sworn in as premier in 1995.

PUBLIC ADMINISTRATION

Luxembourg's government acts through ministerial departments and public authorities directly answerable to it. Each member of the government is in charge of one or more ministerial departments, assisted by advisers.

Certain public services, such as tax collection, the post office, and the water authority, are separate from the central offices of the government. They come under the direction of heads of administration, although still supervised by the minister concerned.

LOCAL GOVERNMENT

Luxembourg is divided into communes, something like states, each administered by a council elected by the people. Council members are elected for six years. From their membership, an executive body is formed to administer the daily affairs of the commune, such as education, public health, and electricity.

LAW OF THE LAND

The exercise of judicial power rests with the courts of law and is completely independent of the executive and legislative branches. Judges of the lower courts, justices of the peace, are directly appointed by the grand duke. There are two branches of jurisdiction in Luxembourg: the judicial order and the administrative order. The administrative courts are designated by the constitution to deal with administrative- and finance-related cases. The judicial order has jurisdiction over minor cases in civil and commercial matters.

The Constitutional Court ranks at the top of the judicial hierarchy. The court is composed of nine members and sits in Luxembourg City. It rules on the conformity of laws with the constitution, except for those laws approving treaties.

The jury system is not used in Luxembourg. Instead, there is a panel of an odd number of judges. A defendant is acquitted if a majority of the presiding judges finds him or her not guilty. A public prosecutor's department represents the state in the courts and acts under the authority of the minister of justice. Assisting them in their work is the police force, which is responsible for investigating crimes and delivering suspects to the courts, under the supervision of the attorney general.

THE ROYAL FAMILY

The crown of the grand duchy is hereditary in the House of Nassau-Weilburg and passes by lineal descent through the male heir. Only if there is no male issue in either of the two branches of the family does the crown pass to the female heir of the reigning dynasty. The endurance of the monarchy is seen by Luxembourgers as a testament of stability and continuity. Widely admired and popular, the royal family live quiet

SYMBOLS OF THE STATE

The coat of arms of Luxembourg was decided upon between 1235 and 1239 by Count Henry V with a design of cross bars of silver and blue, and a red lion rampant—rearing up on hind legs—crowned with gold. On June 23, both the National Day holiday and the grand duke's birthday are celebrated. Luxembourg's flag, with its three horizontal bands of red, white, and blue, is distinguishable from that of the Netherlands only by the shade of its blue—sky blue as opposed to the Dutch ultramarine blue.

The national anthem is the first and last verses of the song "Ons Hémecht" (ONS he-MECHT), "Our Motherland," composed in 1864 with words by Luxembourger Michel Lentz (1820–93). Far from being a martial song, as with many countries, the Luxembourgian national anthem issues a vibrant appeal for peace.

O Thou above, whose powerful hand
Makes States or lays them low,
Protect this Luxembourger land
From foreign yoke and woe.
Your spirit of liberty bestow
On us now as of yore.
Let Freedom's sun in glory glow.

and discreet lives with little pomp or headlines. Far from embracing an isolated and grand lifestyle, members of the royal family can be met shopping in the city center, and the members of the youngest generation attend regular primary and secondary schools.

Other reasons for the continued support of the monarchy by an overwhelming majority of the people are nationalistic and economic. For example, though living in exile in London during World War II, the late Grand Duchess Charlotte spoke to her people regularly on radio and became a living symbol of national identity.

At the end of the war, her husband, Prince Felix, and son Jean, who later became the grand duke, entered Luxembourg in uniform with the first American liberators. The involvement of Jean's oldest son, Henri, the current grand duke, in numerous international organizations, and as part of economic missions, also benefits the country's image and results in considerable trade and investment opportunities.

THE POLITICAL DIVIDE

Luxembourg has four main political parties: the Christian Social Party (CSP), the Luxembourg Socialist Workers' Party (LSWP), the Democratic Party (DP), and the Green Alternative Party (GAP).

The Roman Catholic-oriented CSP has been the dominant partner in governing coalitions. CSP enjoys popular support and strongly backs NATO. CSP leader and current prime minister Jean-Claude Juncker, born in 1954, is seen by many Luxembourgers as a dynamic young man with new ideas and greater vitality than his predecessor. Prior to Juncker, the DP was the only party to have provided a prime minister since World War II. The DP and the LSWP have alternated as junior coalition partners to the ruling party. DP's current president is Claude Meisch, who took over from Lydie Polfer in 2004.

The DP is the oldest political party in Luxembourg, drawing support from the professions and urban middle class. It advocates both social legislation and minimum governmental involvement in the economy and is also pro-NATO. From 1999 to 2004, it was the second largest party in the Chamber of Deputies of Luxembourg, with 15 of the 60 seats. In the 2004 elections, the DP lost five seats, bringing its total down to 10. The rise of single-issue politics, such as better social security treatment, has made life difficult for the traditional opposition, while benefiting those parties more on the fringes of such issues.

Industrial workers who favor strong social legislation support the LSWP, which is moderately pro-NATO. The GAP, officially formed in 1983, has built up its parliamentary seats to seven because environmental consciousness has grown strongly over the past two decades. The Green vote in the European elections was 15 percent in Luxembourg. The party opposes nuclear weapons and nuclear power as well as Luxembourg's

Luxembourg's national flag is similar to the Netherlands' because from 1815 to 1890 the hereditary rulers of the Netherlands' House of Nassau were also the grand dukes of Luxembourg. The use of the lighter shade of blue was made official only in 1981.

military policies, including its membership in NATO. The rise of the Greens along with the collapse of the communist system in eastern Europe spelled the effective demise of the Communist Party, which lost its single remaining seat in the last election.

WOMEN IN POLITICS

A number of women have contributed significantly to politics in Luxembourg, with a few achieving high office, such as Colette Flesch, born in 1937, and Lydie Polfer, born in 1952. Flesch was mayor of Luxembourg City for 10 years, from 1970–80. She was also minister of foreign affairs, minister of economy, and minister of justice during the 1980s. Lydie Polfer, in addition to being both mayor of Luxembourg City (1982–99) and president of the Democratic Party, is also a member of the European Parliament.

Pedestrians could not miss seeing a poster proclaiming "Yes to the constitution" posted just before a referendum on the European Union constitution in Luxembourg in 2005.

A SMALL ARMY

Luxembourg has no compulsory military service, but as a NATO member, it has a contingent of soldiers recruited on a voluntary basis. Women serve in various positions in the military, with many taking on administrative jobs. After three years of active service, soldiers leave the army and are guaranteed jobs in the police force or postal service. A reserve force can be called up in times of international crisis. The army is under civilian control and the command of the grand duke.

ECONOMY

LUXEMBOURG ENJOYS ONE OF THE highest standards of living in the world. In 2003 its gross domestic product (GDP) per capita was 52,200 euros ($71,200), compared with 33,500 euros ($45,700) in the United States and an average of 24,300 euros ($33,200) in Europe. In 2006 its GDP per capita was 52,800 euros ($71,400) and GDP was $34 billion. It is a prosperous country with a highly industrialized and export-intensive economy. The discovery of iron ore in the 1850s marked a turning point in its economy. Until World War I, steelmaking accounted for almost 60 percent of the country's economy. The steel industry's favorable development up to the mid-1970s was also accompanied by growth in the financial and commercial sectors.

Because of many years of prudent financial management, the government's public debt is minimal.

A SUCCESS STORY

The industry and commerce of Luxembourg profit from an ideal geographical location in the center of Europe. This has been exploited to good advantage. Important international cities, as well as major conurbations—continuous strings of urban communities such as the expanding Saar-Lorraine-Luxembourg superregion and the Boston-New York-Washington, D.C. corridor—are situated in the immediate proximity. In the last century, the great transportation links with neighboring countries gave impetus to the steel industry, which helped propel Luxembourg to affluence. Steel from Luxembourg is used all over the world in the building of bridges, skyscrapers, and railways.

Liberal taxation laws as well as legally embedded banking secrecy have encouraged the rapid development of Luxembourg's financial sector. Social stability has brought the country considerable foreign investment and contributed to the general welfare, with unemployment remaining low. In 2006 the country's unemployment rate was 4.1 percent.

Opposite: **Luxembourgers enjoy shopping in a colorful outdoor street market.**

The construction industry suffered a general decline in the early 1990s.

WORKFORCE

Luxembourg employs a large number of "cross-border" and foreign workers. Both lower- and higher-skilled labor is recruited, mostly from Belgium, Germany, and France. Luxembourgers account for only 36 percent of the domestic salaried employment, while cross-border and resident foreign workers account for 37 and 27 percent, respectively. The country's unemployment rate is low compared with the rest of the European countries. The steady increase in employment has, however, slowed in the past few years.

The low unemployment rate is due mainly to a number of public measures enacted to combat unemployment, like early retirement plans and supported training projects for laid-off steel workers. Also, the government's policy of attracting new firms to settle in Luxembourg, especially in the banking and other service sectors, has been successful.

The economic development of Luxembourg over the last 20 years has been marked by a rapid change in the main types of employment. Focus has shifted to the services sector, such as banking, insurance, distributive trades, and communications. At the same time, manufacturing has been diversified.

SOCIAL CONSENSUS

One of the keys to the economic success story has been social consensus. To avoid conflicts among the many different nationalities in the country, it is often necessary to hammer out agreements. The close links that exist between the inhabitants of a small nation make it easier to find solutions on the basis of a national consensus. Although compromise usually costs everyone a little and never makes anyone entirely happy, it seems to have worked as a strategy.

For more than 25 years, economic problems have been dealt with by what is known as the Luxembourg Model. Consultation between the government and employees takes place on many different levels on committees and councils through a tripartite system, involving an official board made up of employer, trade union, and governmental representatives. Such a nonconfrontational approach to industrial relations and negotiations has so far sidestepped major disputes.

A general minimum wage to combat poverty has been in existence since 1945. All wage earners benefit from a salary scale whereby each increase of the level of prices leads to an automatic adjustment

Because of its steel industry, which uses as much as 90 percent of the country's total coal consumption, Luxembourg's per capita energy requirement is over twice that of Belgium.

Today, fewer workers are employed in industries like manufacturing. Luxembourg's continued growth will depend on further diversification of its economy into emerging sectors such as media and communications.

STRIVING FOR QUALITY, SKILL, AND FLEXIBILITY

Because Luxembourg is unable to compete with large producers of consumer goods, it has specialized in market areas where it is important to be the best rather than the biggest.

An example is the case of Sisto Armaturen S.A., a company of 90 employees. It concentrates on the manufacture of diaphragm valves, a product that has many applications, as in microphones and loudspeakers. Customers admire the exceptional quality of Sisto products, and the small company is now recognized as one of the world's specialists in this field.

Another illustration is Ceratizit S.A, which produces hard metal. With its products so widely distributed, there is a good possibility that anyone holding a ballpoint pen at this moment has one with the ball made by Ceratizit. The company leads world production, producing 3.5 billion balls a year! It also undertakes intensive research to maintain its technical advantage.

of salaries, pensions, and allowances. Thus the purchasing power of consumers is safeguarded.

AN EYE FOR OPPORTUNITIES

Luxembourgers have prospered by being quick to identify opportunities for their economy and to exploit market gaps. The banking service, in particular, is a good example. Luxembourg's freedom to maneuver as a tiny state inside the large EU is also important. It can attract business by offering special privileges that its larger neighbors will not or cannot give.

Equally important, Luxembourg has elected political leaders who know how to diversify a small economy by attracting investment and finding lucrative service industries, while preserving a good social climate. As a result, Luxembourg has, in recent decades, become a pioneer of the Eurobond market, a launchpad for the cable and satellite television business through the lure of deregulation, and a prime personal finance center with customized banking services and tax-efficient investment. Major international concerns have established new subsidiaries or expanding existing plants. Luxembourg is host to an

array of Euro institutions, including the European Court of Justice, the European Investment Bank, the Court of Auditors, the administrative center of the European Parliament, and other lucrative earners and spenders clustered together in the popular capital city.

INDUSTRY

Industry, including mining, manufacturing, and construction, is one of the two main sectors of the economy. The other is the banking sector. Iron and steel once were the dominant forces in the economy—from the late 19th century until the crippling steel industry crisis in 1975. That industry has, nonetheless, now been completely restructured, albeit with major cutbacks in jobs. The nation's steel company, ARBED, merged with Aceralia and Usinor in 2002 to form Arcelor. In 2006 the company again merged, with the world's largest steelmaker, Mittal, forming Arcelor-Mittal.

This step, accompanied by modernization of the manufacturing structure, assured that iron and steel remain the country's main industry,

At successful Luxembourgian companies such as Elth S.A., which manufactures thermostats used in washing machines and other consumer goods, employees work around the clock in shifts so that their products are available at the moment they are called for.

despite dwindling iron resources and reduced demand for Luxembourg's steel exports.

Iron and steel currently accounts for 29 percent of all goods exported (excluding services). It provides employment for 22 percent of the industry and 4 percent of the total workforce. Industry contributes about 13 percent of Luxembourg's GDP.

TRADE FAIRS

Luxembourg has a centuries-old tradition of trade fairs dating back to the Middle Ages. Its central geographical position, financial advantages, and liberal commercial regulations continue to attract merchants and purveyors from all over Europe.

Fairs are held annually in the spring and the autumn. The spring fair concentrates on foodstuffs, beverages, sports, and leisure, and draws some 100,000 visitors. The autumn fair is devoted to home building, furnishings, craft products, and machinery. Valuable antiques, contemporary art, and books are also exhibited each year.

Running parallel with the International Pedigree Dog Show is the Dogexpo, where commercial enterprises display everything needed by man for his four-legged friends. Every four years the gastronomic trade show Expogast, which has gained a coveted world-class reputation, takes place.

All the fairs and specialized trade exhibitions take place in the huge Trade Fair and Congress Center. This complex contains 24 halls linked by covered passageways. Simultaneous translation facilities, projection rooms, amplification equipment, and fax services are provided for exhibitors, as well as parking for 2,500 vehicles, and

A car show in Luxembourg. In addition to the regular trade fairs, there are many other shows, such as the Ecology Show, Road Safety, and the Furniture Show.

two restaurants accommodating 800 people. The entire infrastructure is ideal for conferences or trade shows of any kind.

FINANCIAL SERVICES

During the global recession in the 1980s and 1990s, financial services was the only sector in Luxembourg that sustained economic growth. The grand duchy is now the world's second most important center for collective investment undertakings, after the United States, managing over 1,000 billion euros in assets. In 2004 there were some 170 banks from 26 different countries. The banking sector employs some 10 percent of the total workforce, and contributes about 25 percent of Luxembourg's GDP.

One of the main reasons for the growth of Luxembourg as a financial center, apart from the linguistic abilities of Luxembourgers, are the laws concerning taxation. Luxembourg does not tax the interest earned in foreigners' accounts and has strict rules of banking secrecy.

For thousands of wealthy Europeans, who prefer not to pay taxes on their moneys at their own country's top rates, it is a pleasant outing to drive to Luxembourg and have a good lunch after depositing funds in a bank. This is simpler than a trip to the Cayman Islands, for example, and financially safer, because Luxembourg is part of a single market with the euro as its currency. No taxation is the first wall of the fortress. The inner wall is banking secrecy.

While banks are obliged to check the origin of funds, they are not compelled to disclose such information, except when judicial procedures have been initiated. In addition, all countries other than Luxembourg impose controls on the ability of banks to generate profit.

These practices, which give Luxembourg its reputation as a tax haven, have prompted other EU countries to try to introduce European

In recent years, Luxembourg has also become a center for the cross-border life insurance industry.

THE EUROPEAN INVESTMENT BANK

The European Investment Bank, based in Luxembourg, finances a broad spectrum of projects, from major infrastructure to small businesses, as long as they further European integration. Its role is bringing people closer together, stimulating trade, and building up links between Europe's regions, while also observing the rules of rigorous banking practice.

Money has been lent, at a fixed-rate and low interest, for major road, highway, and rail links and for air transportation and telecommunications systems across Europe. There has also been funding for advanced technology, such as aeronautical engineering. A large amount of money is funneled into environmental protection, like waste and sewage treatment plants. Last are the important energy projects, particularly those that are developing alternative sources of energy, like wind farms.

The European Investment Bank maintains a very sound capital base and funds its lending through bond issues.

legislation to end such tax advantages. The Bank of Credit and Commerce International, based in Luxembourg, was shut down in 1991 by international regulators who believed it was involved in illegal activities. Any moves to change the laws, however, have always been successfully blocked by Luxembourg, whose revenues depend heavily on the ongoing profitability of its banks.

AGRICULTURE

The agricultural industry, which includes forestry and fishing, has continued to decline in economic importance since the beginning of industrialization in the early 19th century. Luxembourg's agricultural industry's share of the GDP fell from 4 percent in 1980 to 2 percent in 1985 and 0.6 percent in 2001. In 2006 it contributed only 1 percent to the national income.

About 92 percent of land use in Luxembourg is for agricultural purposes and wooded areas. The principal crops are grains, potatoes, and wine grapes. Substantial numbers of cattle, pigs, and poultry are also raised. The amount of land committed to forestry has actually increased over

the years, and the cultivation of the main types of trees, coniferous and broad-leaved, has also increased.

Some 1 percent of the land is used for grapevine growing. The valley of the Moselle River enjoys a mild climate and ideal soil, lime, and clay, all which make this region highly suited for producing white wines. It is very similar to the Champagne region of France.

Luxembourg's wine industry rests on two keystones. First is the establishment of six cooperative cellars between 1921 and 1948. All of these producers have now combined under an umbrella organization to improve production. For example, the merged vineyard slopes are now efficiently cultivated, compared with what could be done with the former small and irregular parcels of land.

Second, a national wine label stamped on every bottle by the state institution of viticulture guarantees the authenticity and quality of the wines. This national mark acts both as a stimulus to wine producers to create wines of ever higher quality and offers consumers a guarantee that they are getting a first-class wine.

A considerable amount of money is needed to set up a farm, and Luxembourgers regard farming as a very hard way to make a living, with early mornings and long days.

Seasonal grape picking is performed in the Moselle valley from mid-September to the end of October.

TOURISM

The spectacular forests and river valleys of Luxembourg are unmatched, in such a small area, anywhere else in Europe. It is the variety of landscape, combined with castles, picturesque market towns, sunny vineyards, varied cuisines, and archaeological remains that has fostered the tourist industry.

The economic recession in Europe during the 1980s and 1990s has, however, reduced the number of tourists. People began finding it difficult to afford holidays, and, with the brief two-month span of the tourist season, that meant shutting down a number of hotels. Another factor is that many visitors prefer the sunny weather of the Mediterranean to the rainy climate of Luxembourg. Such competition close at hand makes it difficult for those working in the tourist industry.

IRON IN THE FIRE

The Celts and Romans first mastered the production of iron about 1000 B.C. But it was not until the 1850s that the Luxembourgian horizon became lined with blast furnace stacks spewing out clouds of rust-colored fumes. The development of the iron industry brought affluence to the country, and villages changed into towns.

The reign of iron lasted for more than a century, until 1975 and the onset of the world crisis in the iron and steel industry. Mining activities wound down, coming to a standstill in the early 1980s. Now many of the mining galleries have been turned into museums.

EXPORTS AND IMPORTS

Luxembourg's principal exports are steel, wine, farm produce, equipment, textiles, and quarried stone. Main imports are machinery and electrical equipment, base metals, and fuels. Exports and imports of products are mainly to and from neighboring European countries, especially Belgium, Germany, and France.

As a small nation with a high standard of living, Luxembourg can produce only a small part of what it requires. Since its production is fairly specialized, it must sell abroad most of the goods and services it produces. Other members of the EU account for most of Luxembourg's foreign trade.

Luxembourgian and Belgian foreign trade statistics are merged because the two countries are joined in an economic union.

ENERGY

Over half of Luxembourg's energy comes from hydroelectric installations, with the rest from thermal power sources. Apart from the two dams on the Upper Sûre River, an important development in this field has been the construction of a hydroelectric power station on the Our River. Its total production of electricity has doubled in 10 years.

Since 1972, large quantities of natural gas have become available as a result of an agreement with Belgium.

ENVIRONMENT

IN RECENT YEARS PUBLIC OPINION in Luxembourg has swung dramatically in favor of a more dynamic environmental policy, and, through special interest groups, ceaseless pressure is being exerted on the government. The Green Alternative Party has been an influential force in national affairs to the extent that the majority of Luxembourgers are willing to forgo higher living standards if it means keeping their country clean. Environmental politics have come of age with the authorities' trying to introduce a more comprehensive approach to environmental planning, hoping to counter the most pressing threats.

Like most European countries, Luxembourg has not escaped air and water pollution in urban areas, but as a member of the European Union (EU), the nation participates in European initiatives to protect the environment. The EU Environment Council is responsible for ensuring that the environmental perspective is given proper consideration in international projects and economic activities and at all levels of government. The council is formed of EU ministers for the environment, and meetings are held formally four times a year and informally twice more a year.

CLIMATE CHANGE

The historic Kyoto Protocol of the United Nations was adopted during the Luxembourgian presidency of the EU in 1997. Its goal is to combat climate change through global cooperation to reduce greenhouse gas emissions. Luxembourg has the most ambitious reduction target among the EU countries (a reduction of 28 percent by 2008 to 2012). This target was achieved in 1995 because of a significant economic move by the country—the steel industry moved away from blast furnaces to electrical steelworks. Since 2002, however, the country has been stuck above the agreed reduction target due to rising transportation emissions and the

Opposite: **Environmental activists from Greenpeace protested in Luxembourg against logging activities in Asia while European Union ministers met in the city in 2005.**

Dryness of German-Luxembourgish frontier river Sauer.

Large agricultural projects requiring aid from EU common funds are now subject to environmental impact assessments. Also in effect are various restrictions regarding new zones of economic activity.

starting up of the country's first gas-heat cogeneration power plant. Domestic emissions, however, are stable because of a policy promoting the use of renewable energy by agriculture and the private household sectors.

The Ministry of Environment is responsible for policies on air pollution and the greenhouse effect, and its policy on air protection (under the National Plan for Sustainable Development) aims to limit pollution through preventive measures that are both technically and economically feasible. Emission limits are set for all operational engines, and road vehicles are required to undergo regular technical inspection for engine, noise, and gas-emission performance. The ministry also offers economic incentives to the population at large to limit air pollution: an annual road tax for private cars is calculated on engine capacity; and companies investing in antipollution equipment and energy-saving technology are entitled to subsidies of up to 25 percent of the capital cost of such devices.

WASTE MANAGEMENT

An extensive framework of laws and regulations govern Luxembourg's waste management. These policies initially focused on disposal but now emphasize recovery and reduction, and define a waste-management hierarchy. Waste is classified into five separate categories—household, industrial, inert, hospital, and sewage. The strategy for managing waste is to recover and reuse as much as possible. As a result, mobile and permanent collection sites can be found all over the country. Separate collection bins are allocated to paper, glass, bulky items, and organic waste, as well as recoverable metal and plastic items.

A pile of cars scrap destined for recycling.

Several communes operate a harmonized charging system that involves identifying the owners of trash cans by using microchips; mobile collection of three types of waste, which are charged at different rates (final, organic, and paper); and removal of bulky trash on request. In these communes, the volume of waste has been reduced by 50 percent.

A substantial portion of household organic waste and waste from highway and park maintenance is dealt with by composting at three centers serving 57 percent of the population. To achieve 80 percent recovery by 2010, two more facilities are planned, and individual home composting is being encouraged.

BIODIVERSITY

Despite its small size, Luxembourg is home to a fairly wide range of species and habitats. As in most countries, however, human activities such as agriculture, urbanization, transportation, and tourism are increasingly impacting the countryside in general and many natural or seminatural ecosystems in particular.

Out of the 60-odd mammalian species, over half are threatened, yet others are thriving. The otter has disappeared from the rivers; populations of the badger, on the other hand, which were decimated by gassing during a period of rabies control, have been restored. The wildcat is still present in the Ardennes and in abandoned open-pit mines in the south.

There are 129 nesting bird species. Of these, some 50 percent are threatened. Several bird species, such as the marsh harrier, the peregrine falcon, the black grouse, the hoopoe, the crested lark, and the tawny pipit, disappeared in the 1960s. The black stork has reappeared and is nesting in the Belgian and Luxembourgian plateau of the Ardennes.

Small game hunting is permitted, though the number of species classified as game by law is few. Sadly, game hunting for larger animals such as stags, roe deer, and wild boar, which depend on forest habitat, is on the increase.

Left: **The black stork is one of the precious bird species that can still be sighted in Luxembourg. However, its survival depends on the sustainability of the environment the country and its neighbors have to offer.**

Opposite: **A sighting of the red deer in Luxembourg's forest. Increasing urbanization, commercial logging, and hunting pose a serious threat to the natural habitats of Luxembourg's wildlife and the survival of animals such as the deer.**

LAND AND WATER HABITAT

Forest covers approximately 35 percent of the country. The Ardennes region is the most heavily forested area. Beech and oak are the most common trees found in much of the forestland, though there are other types of woods that attract attention for their rarity and for the flora and fauna found in them. These include ravine forests of maple, pine, swampy alder stands, and peaty birch woods. Luxembourg's forests are made accessible by the public road network and are open to the public.

Apart from the Chiers River, which flows toward France and forms part of the Meuse basin, all the rivers are part of the Moselle subbasin, which empties into the Rhine River. While the density of the rivers and streams is highest in the narrow valleys of the Ardennes, the rivers and streams in Gutland in the south wind mostly through agricultural valleys.

PROTECTING THE ENVIRONMENT

The Water and Forest Administration has been in charge of nature conservation since 1965. The 1965 Nature Protection Act was passed to protect landscapes and the rural environment. It reflected an emerging awareness of the negative impact of uncontrolled building development on city outskirts and the urbanization of the countryside. The farsighted act was amended three times, in 1978, 1982, and in 1992.

The objectives of the act are to conserve the natural environment by protecting and restoring natural areas and landscapes; to protect flora and fauna, and their biotopes—their natural regions; to maintain and improve biological balances; to protect natural resources from damage of all kinds; and to improve the structures of the natural environment.

Several nongovernmental organizations (NGOs) are also actively involved in protecting species through specific programs. The oldest

THE KYOTO PROTOCOL

The Kyoto Protocol, named after the Japanese town of Kyoto where the treaty was written, was adopted by governments from 37 industrialized countries in December 1997 to tackle the issue of climate change. Building on the outline of the United Nations Framework Convention on Climate Change (UNFCCC), the protocol sets legally binding limits on greenhouse gas emissions from, originally, all member states of the European Union except Cyprus and Malta, which did not join the EU until 2004, as well as from the EU as one single body (known as the EU-15, since it then had only 15 member countries). It also introduces innovative market-based implementation mechanisms— the so-called Kyoto flexible mechanisms—aimed at keeping the cost of curbing pollutant emissions low.

Under the Kyoto Protocol, industrialized countries are required to reduce their emissions of six greenhouse gases by around 5 percent below the 1990 level during the first Kyoto Protocol "commitment period" from 2008 to 2012. A five-year commitment period was chosen rather than a single target year to smooth out annual fluctuations in emissions due to such uncontrollable factors as weather. There are no emission targets for developing countries. Penalties can be levied for noncompliance.

The Kyoto Protocol, which entered into force on February 16, 2005, requires that at least 55 parties to the UNFCCC ratify the protocol and that they include industrialized countries accounting for at least 55 percent of the industrialized countries' carbon dioxide emissions in 1990—this took a while to achieve.

As of April 18, 2006, 162 nations and the European Community had ratified the protocol. Two countries that originally signed the treaty did not ratify: the United States rejected the protocol, whereas Australia decided not to ratify it. This means there are 36 developed countries and the EU-15 as an entity that are obliged to reach their Kyoto targets.

association is the LNVL or the National League for the Protection of Nature and Birds. Other associations indirectly involved in environmental management include the Luxembourg Hunting Federation, the Saint Hubert Club, the Luxembourg Anglers' Federation, and the Luxembourg Naturalists' Society. The latter is actively engaged in research and has close links with the Natural History Museum.

LUXEMBOURGERS

SINCE THE BEGINNING of its industrialization, Luxembourg has sustained a strong growth in population. This is because of continuous immigration since the end of the 19th century. In 1990 Luxembourg had a population of about 200,000. Today, in the early 21st century, this number has more than doubled to more than 481,000.

POPULATION TRENDS

In spite of the conspicuous total growth, the overall trend nowadays is a falling birthrate—with the population growing at less than 1 percent annually—and an aging population. The little real growth that has occurred over the last 30 years has come about only because of migration.

Immigrants make up a significant percent of the population—39 percent in 2004. In percentage terms, there are more foreigners in Luxembourg than in any other country in the European Union. Despite this large newcomer presence, there are few problems arising from this, and the population lives well in multicultural coexistence.

According to studies carried out by sociologists, 30 percent of the country's passport holders have at least one parent of foreign origin. If the grandparents' generation is included, the proportion increases to 45 percent. Historically, the largest group of immigrants were the Germans, who account for 12 percent, followed by the French (11 percent), the Italians (9 percent), and the Belgians (6 percent). The highest concentration of immigrants is in the steelmaking area of Minette, in the south, where every second resident is from an immigrant family, the majority from Italy.

Above: **The Luxembourger's slightly unconventional character is the result of centuries of intense relations with the cultures and peoples of neighboring nations.**

Opposite: **Luxembourgers taking a break at the Place du Marche (Market Square) at Echternach.**

57

Senior citizens enjoying a good joke and leisure time in a neighborhood park. Luxembourger hospitality is renowned. Sir Winston Churchill once described Luxembourg as the country that charmed him most and "where hospitality has been most simple and cordial."

NATIONAL PRIDE

Luxembourgers are the result of the merging of two quite distinct cultures: in the west is the French group to which Luxembourg is linked by its civilization, and in the east is the Germanic group to which the country belongs linguistically. From the end of the third century, migrations of Germanic tribes began settling in the region of Luxembourg. All this resulted in a national character based on its ability to enrich itself from other cultures and a genuine desire to mix foreign contributions with its own heritage.

Citizens do not fear losing their Luxembourgian identity because they see themselves as completely different from both the Germans and the French. Repeatedly invaded, they have survived, and that has bred their tremendous loyalty. This innate pride and patriotism is easily noticeable today. Delighted to discover the role their nation can play on an international level, as part of a wider Europe, Luxembourgers have gained confidence in their ability as a nation.

CHARACTER AND PERSONALITY

Luxembourgers are known as a friendly, convivial, polite, and open-minded people who have a well-developed sense of hospitality. Many older Luxembourgers are particularly friendly toward visitors from the United States because of the pivotal role American soldiers played in the liberation of their country from the Nazis.

Some regional differences are observed, however. People in the southern part of Luxembourg have a reputation for being outspoken. In the north, Luxembourgers are said to have developed an easygoing joie de vivre because their harsh living conditions have led the locals to take advantage of life's enjoyments as best as they can.

Cautious, hardworking, practical, conservative, and traditional: these are traits often associated with the Luxembourger. In addition, Luxembourgian entrepreneurs are known for their characteristic self-composure in most situations.

Enjoying the pleasures of life, however, is as important to them as work, and with their passion for festivities, Luxembourgers grasp opportunities to celebrate and to organize parades and processions. The national motto, seen carved in stone walls, perhaps best sums up the people's character: "We want to remain what we are."

MELTING POT

In terms of ethnic composition, the greatest groups of immigrants in Luxembourg are Portuguese, Italian, French, Belgian, and German.

The Luxembourgers' ability to compromise can be seen by the successive waves of immigration and the smooth integration of guest workers: Italians in 1870s and the 1920s for the steel industry, and the present surge of Portuguese, which began in the 1960s, especially active in building and construction. A generally positive attitude toward immigrants willing to integrate and pursue culturally similar values has produced a melting pot without threatening national identity. The annual Festival of Immigration attracts the patronage of the highest dignitaries, and the major political parties all emphasize the importance to the country of the presence of nonindigenous people.

In Luxembourg, despite the many different nationalities, there has been little, if any, intolerance or racial unrest. Although a group called the Antiracism and Anti-Semitism Movement of Luxembourg does exist, pointing to some underlying currents of antagonism, attempts to create extreme-right-wing groups have been very short-lived. Any fascist notion is fiercely rejected, because during World War II Luxembourg suffered greatly at the hands of Nazi zealots and the losses were painfully extensive. Hardly a family has not lost some member in

LUXEMBOURGERS IN THE UNITED STATES

It is often said that there are more people of Luxembourgian origin in the United States than there are actually in Luxembourg! This is because in the second half of the 19th century, one out of every five Luxembourgers emigrated to the United States.

The majority now live in Illinois and Iowa, but the first emigrants who left their home country settled in Wisconsin and in Minnesota, where today there are a number of Luxembourgian heritage groups. One village in Iowa looks as if it had been transported brick by brick from Luxembourg. Prominent personalities in the United States of Luxembourgian origin include tennis player Chris Evert; U.S. Olympic gold medalist in decathlon (1932), James Bausch; photographer Edward Steichen; actress Loretta Young; and President Franklin Delano Roosevelt.

the German concentration camps, on the Russian front, or in the Resistance movement.

An important factor that undoubtedly eases integration is the country's low unemployment rate. Social unrest and conflict are less likely to occur where jobs are plentiful and individuals have some control over their destiny.

The problems faced by immigrants are more often of a practical nature, such as housing shortages and language barriers, which hamper many from getting ahead, than overt racism. A young man from Cape Verde who works and lives in Luxembourg and is married to a local woman, says he experiences no difficulty with the fact that he is black and she white. "Everyone is so friendly to me." The disturbing trend toward a "new poverty" among illegal immigrants living in the country is a far greater threat than prejudice.

DRESS

Today it is difficult to find traditional Luxembourgian dress worn just anywhere, for it is likely to be seen only on festive occasions. Women's customary, time-honored dress consists of a full-length royal blue skirt, gathered at the waist, and trimmed with a white border above the hem. Worn over this is a small, semicircular white apron, richly embroidered at the bottom. A long-sleeved, plain white cotton blouse, a red or white cloth bonnet, and a red cloth shawl across the shoulders complete the outfit.

Lighthearted young Luxembourgers find interesting pastimes wherever they gather.

The traditional dress makes a rare appearance at this festive dance.

Flat black shoes and thick white stockings are worn, and a wicker basket is typically carried. When a dance routine, an intrinsic part of the culture for women, is performed, the usual dress is a white blouse with a short black skirt.

Men's traditional dress is a blue tunic in a smock style with a red edging. Black knee-length breeches are worn, together with a white shirt and either a black bow tie or a red scarf. Knee-high socks, black shoes with silver buckles, and a peaked cap finish off the outfit.

For men living in the rural parts of the country and earning their living as farmers, the usual festive costume is a red scarf and short blue overalls.

PROMINENT LUXEMBOURGERS

Despite its small population, the country of Luxembourg has, in recent years, produced several internationally recognized personalities.

A figure of national importance was Joseph Bech (1887–1975), prime minister during World War II. Bech, a modest and discreet man, played a significant role in keeping up the country's morale during the war years and the consequent turmoil. He also made important contributions to the development of the United Nations and a united Europe, sensitive to the gains from integration rather than focusing on strictly national goals.

Robert Schuman (born in Luxembourg in 1886, died 1963) launched the Schuman Plan that led to the establishment of the European Coal and Steel Community, the first step toward European integration. Young Schuman left Luxembourg to study law in Germany and later lived in

CAPE VERDE ISLANDERS

Cape Verde, a nation of islands located off the west coast of Africa, and Luxembourg have developed close economic and humanitarian ties. In 2003 Luxembourg spent more than 8 million euros in development aid for Cape Verde. The archipelago occupies a key position in the grand duchy's European cooperation programs.

In the 1960s, when the first generation of islanders arrived in Luxembourg, Cape Verde was still a Portuguese colony that did not gain independence until 1975. Immigrants went to Portugal first, where they were treated as citizens, and then to Paris and finally Luxembourg, where there was work. Several thousand immigrants from Cape Verde live and work in Luxembourg today. Illegal immigration, nevertheless, is an ongoing practice, with many such newcomers living in the country for over 30 years. With adult children in Luxembourg, it is unlikely now that they would return to Cape Verde.

One certainty is that all of the islanders came to the grand duchy with the hope of a better life, and for many, their dreams have been realized.

France. Elected to the French Parliament in 1919, he fought with the Resistance during World War II and became French foreign minister in the late 1940s. Schuman is seen as the architect of European unification, and his memory is greatly revered in the country of his birth.

Another Luxembourger, Gabriel Lippmann, was a respected scientist and a winner of the Nobel Prize in Physics. Born in 1845, in a small village, he obtained his doctorate in sciences in Paris in 1875. He then focused his research on thermodynamics and electrical instruments and eventually presented to the French academy his method of color photography based on the interference of light waves. In 1908 he was awarded a Nobel Prize for producing the first color photographic plate, an important first step in the development of color photography.

Following in Lippman's footsteps, prominent modern-day scientists from Luxembourg include Claude P. Müller (born 1954), who has been particularly honored by his fellow scientists. Müller specializes in viral immunology and has received considerable recognition for his work in vaccines.

LIFESTYLE

THE OVERWHELMING MAJORITY of Luxembourgers, 70 percent, live in towns, rather than the countryside. Luxembourgian society is both urban and very cosmopolitan, a finding that can sometimes seem at odds with the fact that most of the country's land is used for agriculture.

Although Luxembourg is a small nation, it is not overcrowded. Luxembourgers have ample access to their own space. The pace of life in the capital city can be fast and stressful at times, like any other European capital. Away from the city, though, life is slower and more laid-back.

STANDARD OF LIVING

Luxembourg has the highest standard of living in the EU. Numerous indicators confirm its prosperity. Citizens of the grand duchy receive more social benefits per 1,000 inhabitants than anywhere else in Europe. When prices go up, wages and pensions increase accordingly, so consumers do not feel the pinch.

Only the former West Germany has more cars, Denmark more telephones, and the Netherlands more hospitals. Some 70 percent of Luxembourgers own their homes, and housing standards are high, with all having electricity and running water. Luxembourg has the highest per capita consumption of electricity in Europe.

Factors that contribute to the high quality of life in Luxembourg are an ideal population density and the absence of big cities. Short distances to and from work, combined with adequate transportation facilities, also help make daily life easier.

Above: **A customer gets a makeover in a shopping mall in Luxembourg.**

Opposite: **Urban Luxembourgers take a breather on a sunny afternoon in the city.**

HEARTH AND HOME

Nearly two-thirds of the total population of Luxembourg lives in the 10 major towns, which are also centers of industrial production. About 30 percent of Luxembourgers, 115,000 people, live in just three of these towns. Luxembourg City, the capital, alone has 78,300 inhabitants. Because of exorbitant rents, the center of Luxembourg City sees little activity outside of business hours. Instead, residential neighborhoods have sprung up in the vicinity of the city, neatly separated from industrial areas.

In Luxembourg, as in the rest of Europe, the number of people living in rural areas is fast dwindling. Preserving the rural heritage is a difficult task and the delicate balance between town and country is in some peril. Although the countryside offers abundant recreational activities, rural areas are unable to sustain the level of commerce necessary for a dynamic local community. Infrastructure is often poor and services inadequate compared with urban areas.

COMFORTABLE LIVING

The average Luxembourgian family has a detached two- to three-bedroom house. All have central heating, predominantly by oil, have double-glazed windows, and usually include such features as marble counters and wooden parquet floors. Gardens and flowers are important to Luxembourgers. For people without a garden, colorful window boxes are the next best thing. (*Pictured here are the hillside houses of Luxembourg's Montee de la Petrusse*).

FAMILY VALUES

Luxembourgers have strong traditional values. Families are very important to most people and are woven into a significant part of the social fabric. Boarding schools are quite rare, and every opportunity is taken to spend time with the family—even lunch breaks.

Still, changes are taking place, even in small towns and villages where conservatism and a reluctance to change is often entrenched. As women become more active in the working life, many are delaying marriage and childbearing. This is a fundamental social change, which neighboring countries have experienced for a much longer time. Nevertheless, over 95 percent of Luxembourgian women rate their families as their top priority, and few place careers before their families.

Political stability and economic prosperity have helped make Luxembourg—in the words of former United Nations Secretary-General Perez de Cuellar—"one of the world's happiest nations."

WOMEN

Women account for about 40 percent of the working population in Luxembourg. They largely dominate the health and social work sector, education, real estate, and domestic workers employed by householders. The motivation for working is usually to provide a higher standard of living for her family. A growing proportion of women now bring in at least half the household income.

The lack of child-care facilities has curtailed the entry of more women into the workforce. At present, there is public provision of child-care services for fewer than 5 percent of children up to 3 years old. Luxembourg is one of only three countries in Western Europe without a statutory paternity allowance.

With the growing dominance of the service industries, more job opportunities have been created for women. Nonetheless, women remain underrepresented in industry and the professions, despite laws that ensure equal access to employment and equal pay, training, and working conditions.

YOUNG PEOPLE

Demographic change in the country has resulted in the fact that in the last 10 years the number of adolescents in Luxembourg has been declining. A major worry facing these young people—and this is not unique to Luxembourg—is jobs and careers. A study conducted in 2000, "Youth Policy in Luxembourg," found that 32 percent of young people age 12–25 in Luxembourg were employed. The findings revealed that young people are entering the labor market later, as they prolong their educations. Wages of young people, compared with adults' salaries, are falling, a trend also found elsewhere in Europe. The "traditional" youth labor-market's recruiting among school dropouts is shrinking, and the jobs available in it are increasingly likely to be low paid and dead-end.

Youth centers in Luxembourg, often called Maisons des jeunes (Mjs) provide a range of daytime and evening activities, mainly for teenagers, usually young males. Typical organized activities include audiovisual initiatives that allow young people to make films about their communities, and training on the use of the Internet.

While Luxembourgers have managed to fashion a very high standard of living for themselves over the last few decades, the aging population means that younger people will have to bear an increasingly greater burden of maintaining this superior quality of life.

EDUCATION

Primary education begins at age 6 and lasts for six years. At age 12, after taking entrance exams, pupils are assigned to one of three types of secondary schools: grammar (college prep), secondary technical, or complementary education. Each of these has a different curriculum and vocational objectives. Education is compulsory for all until the age of 15.

Students attending grammar school who are successful in the final examination at the age of 18 or 19 can go on to university. Since 2003, Luxembourg has had its own university, with three research-led faculties. Luxembourgers who want to go abroad to study may, of course, still do so.

In the secondary technical system, a student may stay until age 18, leaving with a vocational qualification, an apprenticeship, or a diploma for higher technical studies.

The complementary education course is for students who fail to get into either of the mainstream options. Complementary education classes have come under considerable criticism because they offer poor chances for gaining qualifications and are attended by low achievers, many of whom are young immigrants with inadequate preparation.

Children with physical disabilities receive special education, separate from the mainstream. Many parents disagree with this practice, believing that their disabled child would benefit from being schooled alongside the able-bodied.

THE WELFARE STATE

The low birthrate, relative to the aging population, is of acute concern to everyone responsible for shaping government policy. The average life expectancy has risen from 50 in 1900 to 79 in 2007: 76 for men and 83 for women. The birthrate was about 11.9 per thousand Luxembourgers in 2007. The result is growing numbers of elderly people but fewer people of working age to provide for them. As of 2007, 67 percent of Luxembourg's population is made up of people between the ages of 15 and 64. About 15 percent of Luxembourgers are 65 years old or older.

Governmental statistics in 2007 revealed that about 20.8 percent of the nation's GDP was channeled into social security and welfare services for Luxembourgers.

Maternity benefits are available for women who stay at home after childbirth or adoption for up to four months and are intended to reimburse lost wages.

Economic consequences include increases to the state burden of old-age pensions and sickness benefits. Political consequences arise from finding the money to pay for these growing costs. Thus far, welfare policy in Luxembourg has withstood attempts to cut benefits. Clearly, any move to do so would be very unpopular with the voters.

Social policies are highly developed. All types of employment are subject to compulsory contributory benefits, which is a combination of taxes paid by employees and employers. The resulting comprehensive social insurance plan covers medical and hospital treatments, disability and old-age pensions, family allowances, and unemployment benefits. A major advantage of this system is that everyone receives health-care benefits, unlike in the United States, where basically only the aged and the poor receive governmental help. Hospital treatment is free, but those who can afford better attention from private physicians or hospitals, for example, experience less time waiting for an operation and are free to buy private medical insurance. The number of general physicians, specialists, and available hospital beds have all increased substantially during the last decade.

The family allowance, which most industrialized countries have, with the notable exception of the United States, is a universal cash benefit that goes to every family regardless of income. The government itself does not administer social services. Social services are run by public bodies made up of representatives of the government, employers, and employees.

CRIME AND PUNISHMENT

The police in Luxembourg are armed—as in all European countries except Britain, where only a few officers routinely carry weapons—but their

Police officers provide a reassuring presence on the streets. There were reportedly only 498 prisoners in Luxembourg in 2007, compared with the more than 2 million inmates in the prisons of the United States.

presence on the streets of Luxembourg is not a heavy one. Relationships between the public and the police are generally good, and the powers they possess are not viewed as particularly intrusive or excessive.

For the average law-abiding citizen, the offense most likely to give them food for thought is driving under the influence of alcohol. The maximum permissible blood-alcohol concentration is 80 mg, about 2 units—the same as in the United States—and penalties are high for those who test above that. Punishment can lead to a severe fine, loss of a driver's license for a year, and sometimes imprisonment.

The lifting of European borders has affected crime rates at all levels. Drug-related crime, prostitution, burglaries, and muggings are all increasing, but statistics for violent crime have remained at the same low level.

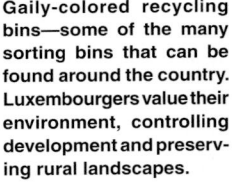

Gaily-colored recycling bins—some of the many sorting bins that can be found around the country. Luxembourgers value their environment, controlling development and preserving rural landscapes.

GREEN LIVING

Much of Luxembourg's charm lies in the variety of its scenery and the many country areas available for recreation. Citizens are vigilant about caring for their surroundings, and litter is rarely, if ever, seen on the streets. But industrialization has caused damage to the environment, and people living in the capital and alongside highways are particularly troubled by noise pollution.

The high density of motor vehicle traffic and the concentration of industry lead to high levels of nitrogen oxides in the air and significant amounts of airborne dust. Air pollution remains below the critical health threshold, but its effects on human health and that of the forests are coming under careful scrutiny. To make matters worse, acid rain is damaging the forests.

Conditions of most rivers are acceptable, but about 4 percent of the watercourses in the center and south of the country are quite heavily polluted. Estuaries, in particular, bear the brunt of man's carelessness. The quality of drinking water is generally satisfactory, but groundwater in some aquifers is threatened, both from an increase in nitrates and decreasing amounts of water available.

Pollution from Luxembourg's factories. The country now has many monitoring sites measuring the amount of nitrogen dioxide in the air.

RELIGION

IN THE PAST, RELIGION was as divisive an issue in Luxembourg as in the rest of Europe. Many battles and massacres took place in the name of religion. Today, over 95 percent of Luxembourgers are Roman Catholic. Any discrimination on the basis of religion is illegal. Luxembourgers remain deeply committed to Catholicism, and their religion is still an important part of their cultural life.

FROM DRUIDISM TO CHRISTIANITY

The Druids were a priestly order who ruled in this area until Roman law, and later Christianity, put an end to their dominance. Little is known about the Druids other than that they were part of an elaborate religious and political organization. Their religion was a cult recognizing numerous gods and natural objects, such as trees and water, in which magical practices were involved. Assemblies were held in consecrated spots, such as groves of oaks. Mistletoe growing on these oaks was venerated and used in medicine.

Christianity was introduced early in Luxembourg, during the third century, but only began to flourish in the seventh century with the arrival of Irish and English missionaries. The Anglo-Saxon priest Saint Willibrord (c. 658–739) converted all of the Low Countries to Christianity. He worked for many years from Echternach, in eastern Luxembourg, from which he spread the message of Catholicism throughout the region. Saint Willibrord was buried in Echternach, where his crypt is still visited. His tomb became one of the most important pilgrimage destinations in the region, with many believing that the aura around the altar of the crypt could cure plague, leprosy, and eye afflictions.

Above: **A hand-colored engraving of Druids harvesting mistletoe to use in their ceremonies, while Roman soldiers keep watch. Today's Christmas tradition of putting up mistletoe dates back to Druid traditions.**

Opposite: **The grand spires and imposing entrance of Cathédrale Notre-Dame, or Notre Dame Cathedral, in Luxembourg City. The Cathédrale Notre-Dame's three spires are today a prominent landmark on the city's skyline. Among those buried within the cathedral's crypt is the revered 14th-century Count of Luxembourg, John the Blind.**

A medieval engraving of a monk meticulously copying a manuscript.

A MEDIEVAL CENTER

During the Middle Ages, learning was concentrated in large monastic centers, where monks preserved important books by carefully copying them, often adding elaborate illustrations. Most of this work of copying was concentrated on the gospels.

One of the most important monastic centers during the early Middle Ages was Echternach. The center is remembered today chiefly for the Echternach Gospels, lavishly decorated 11th-century manuscripts that are some of the best and most treasured examples of medieval manuscript illumination.

The old Benedictine abbey that still stands in Echternach was founded in the seventh century by Saint Willibrord. Known as the Basilica, it has four wings of 230 feet (70 m) each built around a large square courtyard. One of the most important religious buildings in the country, it enshrines a magnificent white sarcophagus holding the remains of Saint Willibrord. The Basilica was partially destroyed during the Battle of the Bulge in 1944, but has now been completely restored.

THE PROTESTANT CHALLENGE

During the Middle Ages, all of Europe was Roman Catholic. But with the spread of the Reformation in the late 15th and early 16th centuries, Protestant beliefs and practices began to spread and slowly dominate. The Reformation, an attempt to reform the Catholic Church, was begun by Martin Luther in 1517. Luther's attacks on issues of doctrine, and the widespread

JESUIT ORDER

The Roman Catholic order of religious men founded by Saint Ignatius Loyola in 1540 has been noted for its educational, missionary, and charitable works in modern times. Saint Ignatius was a noble Spanish soldier who experienced a religious conversion and established the order.

The Society of Jesus grew rapidly and gained a prominent role in the Church, thus exposing it to much hostility. Education and scholarship were their principal works from the beginning. Early Jesuits were also preachers, many entering the foreign missionary field, and were often called upon to be confessors to many of the royal families of Europe.

Jesuits have always been controversial. While some have seen them as the most esteemed religious order, others have regarded them as a devious force to be feared and condemned. In the 15th and 16th centuries, their efforts to become the predominant religious power certainly contributed to the witch hunts and burnings of that period.

Jesuit missionaries arrived in Luxembourg in 1583, and in 1594 set up a grammar school (the present-day national library). In 1621 the construction of the grand Jesuit church Eglise Notre-Dame (Church of Our Lady)—known by the 19th century as Cathédrale Notre-Dame de Luxembourg (the Notre Dame Cathedral of Luxembourg) and located in the heart of the grand duchy's capital—was completed. When the Austrians suppressed the Jesuit Order in 1773, the Jesuits left, gradually making their return to Luxembourg at the end of the 19th century.

corruption in the Catholic Church hierarchy, changed religious practices in Europe. Many breakaway sects grew rapidly and took up revolutionary views, particularly a militant Protestantism called Calvinism.

The Spanish, however, who ruled the Low Countries at that time, were staunch defenders of the Catholic faith. That was also the time of the brutal Inquisition in Spain, when no torture was too terrible to inflict upon dissenters. Widespread resentment at the Spaniards' attempt to hold their subjects submissive to the Roman Catholic Church grew as Protestantism became firmly entrenched elsewhere.

Religious differences flared up between the north and south of the Low Countries when the south (present-day Luxembourg and Belgium) became alarmed at the spread of Lutheranism and Calvinism. The new Protestant doctrines failed to penetrate Luxembourg's borders, which remained Catholic and loyal to Spain. The north, today's Netherlands, became Protestant. All over Europe, rulers had to decide whether to accept or reject this new Christian religion, and this split between Catholicism and Protestantism ravaged Europe for more than a century.

In 1626 there were 15,544 Jesuits worldwide. This increased to 22,589 by 1749. Today there are some 20,000 members. The society's founder, Saint Ignatius Loyola, died in 1556.

WITCHCRAFT

In the duchy between 1588 and 1631, as many as 100 women were victims of witch trials annually. Some men were also accused of practicing the crime of witchcraft. All it took to set the malevolent machinery going was a rumor, often pointing to women living alone or isolated from society, who were felt to be suspicious characters. The ordinances of Philip II of Spain laid down strict procedures in the matter of interrogation and torture. Everything had to be done "through legitimate legal procedures according to the principles of law, honesty, reason, and justice." Unfortunately, not all investigations of witchcraft abided by these humanistic principles.

TRIAL AND EXECUTION

Once a witchcraft trial was underway, accusations against new suspects were often provoked while under torture. The accused witch might exert her vengeance on those who made her suffer by denouncing them as accomplices. Often the charges boiled down to cases of bad reputation and the interpretation of odd behavior. Perhaps the defendant was heard letting out awful shrieks at night, or her envious sister-in-law claimed she had killed one of her babies by looking at it.

Acquittal came if the suspect withstood the torture without confessing, but very often the accused then died afterward from the ill treatment. If the defendant did not confess, there was no proof.

The ritual of execution was the climax of the whole ghastly system. Witchcraft was considered one of the most heinous crimes against God and the king, and the judges needed the spectacle of the stake to confirm the person's guilt and to ignite fear in the citizens' hearts. Everyone had to see the body burning in order to acknowledge the triumph of law. All joined in the execution, with the villagers gathering armfuls of firewood. On the assigned day, a procession of the entire town escorted the prisoner to the place of death. Often the condemned was strangled by the executioner before being completely reduced to ashes. A banquet followed for the local lords and magistrates.

After about 1631, such trials stopped in Luxembourg. Work began on the building of a new society based on law and order, and witchcraft was no longer a preoccupation of the judges.

RELIGION TODAY

Today the population is still overwhelmingly Roman Catholic. When the pope visited the country in 1985, the bishop was elevated to archbishop and placed under the direct authority of the pope without any intermediate hierarchy, a position usually reserved for cardinals. That was an almost unprecedented occurrence, an illustration of how important Luxembourg is to the Roman Catholic Church.

Almost all Protestant churches are represented in Luxembourg, though their influence is small. The evangelicals—believers in the absolute authority of Scripture—have the most followers. There is a notable Jewish community as well.

In Luxembourg, as in most countries in the West, there has been a dramatic decline in the number of people, especially young adults, who

Above: **During the two weeks of the national pilgrimage, the Octave, beginning on the third Sunday after Easter, the Cathédrale Notre-Dame becomes the center of religious life in the country. During this time, large numbers of Luxembourgers flock there to venerate the image of Our Lady, patron saint of the city.**

Opposite: **A 1489 woodcut of witches conjuring up a hailstorm.**

The parish church at Vianden, recently renovated, was built in 1248 in the Gothic style with two naves.

For many centuries, sarcophagi (stone coffins) were the main form of interment for a deceased person. The word sarcophagus comes from Greek words meaning "flesh-eating stone." During the rule of the Roman Empire, the sides of coffins were carved with various pictures, often of battle scenes, gods and goddesses, vines and flowers, and so forth. Sometimes the recumbent figure of the deceased was carved on the lid. Beautiful sarcophagi can be seen in churches and museums around the world.

attend a church of any denomination. Despite the residual influence of the Catholic Church, the birthrate is one of the lowest in the world, and the number of divorces has soared. Recruitment of clergy, like church attendance, is also decreasing rapidly. Nevertheless, the Church still fills an important place in the lives of most Luxembourgers.

Despite a decline in church attendance among young people, politics and religion are deeply entwined, and the church dominates many facets of life, including the media and education. The conservative party is intimately linked with the Roman Catholic Church. One influential daily newspaper, the *Luxemburger Wort*, is the official publication of the Christian Social Party and the Catholic Church. Royal family members are all devout Catholics.

Relations between church and state are governed by law. All clergy of the officially recognized churches are paid by the state, giving them a civil service status, although they are appointed by their particular religious authority. Religion is a compulsory subject in schools, although a special course on morality and social studies was introduced as an alternative some years ago. School holidays are determined by religious holidays.

PLACES OF WORSHIP

A main center for Luxembourg's Catholics is the Cathedral of Our Lady, known as the Cathédrale Notre-Dame. Built as a Jesuit church between 1613 and 1621, in the Gothic manner, with a Renaissance door, it was enlarged in 1935 with the addition of impressive spires. Noteworthy inside are the massive pillars, with strikingly original ornamentation, and magnificent sculptures and statues.

There is also a crypt containing the burial vaults of various members of the grand ducal family and important bishops. Access to the crypt, which has 12 columns supporting the church above, is by a staircase guarded by two bronze lions bearing the arms of the House of Luxembourg.

Other places of worship in the capital city include the Church of Saint Michael from the 10th century, the Chapel of Saint Quirin (14th century), the Church of Saint John upon the Stone (17th century), and the Protestant church from the 18th century.

The countryside is dotted with churches and chapels. The most prominent ones are located in the north, such as in the village of Heiderscheidergrund. The chapel there has a unique octagonal shape called an "inkpot." Built in 1850, it is dedicated to Saint Kunigunda, who is represented in a statue above the door and in a stained-glass window.

The exquisite and elegant interior of the Cathédrale Notre-Dame.

Inside the chapel in the town of Esch-sur-Sûre there is an imposing life-size carving of the Gothic Calvary (Christ on the cross and the two thieves). It is one of the most important cultural treasures of the country.

At another village, Bavigne, during World War II, the villagers made a pledge to build a chapel to Our Lady if they survived the Nazi occupation. Since 1953, the hilltop behind the town has been dominated by three huge oak crosses and the pledged chapel, with a cherished statue of Our Lady on a stone pedestal.

Echternach remains an important religious center. An open-air Mass is celebrated at Echternach each year on Whitsunday to venerate the relics there of Saint Willibrord.

 **TRIER** 46
SAARBRUCKEN 145

 **E29 ECHTERNACH** 35

 **E421 ETTELBRUCK** 29

AUTRES DIRECTIONS

LANGUAGE

THE NATIONAL LANGUAGE OF Luxembourg is Luxembourgish (LUX-em-borg-gish), or Lëtzebuergish (LET-zen-borg-ish). Like Flemish, it is an offshoot of one of the many branches of the Germanic languages. Luxembourgers, however, do not like their tongue to be confused with German.

During the Nazi occupation in 1941, the people voted by an overwhelming 96 percent in a referendum to convey to their oppressors that their language was not German, but Luxembourgish. After the war the public use of Luxembourgish increased dramatically as a natural reaction against four years of suppression. It eventually came to win its full right of use in the grand duchy.

As a country straddling the linguistic frontier, Luxembourg has always represented a meeting place of the cultural and political worlds of both France and Germany. Not surprisingly, French and German are spoken fluently alongside the national language. Each language has a distinct function within the Luxembourgian society.

RIVALRY OF LANGUAGES

While naturally proud of their own language, Luxembourgers realize they are in a unique position, wherein French and German are equally important. Still, they consider it common courtesy for people to try to speak the national language of a country that they are in, especially when working there.

Consequently, anger is sometimes felt when workers from across the border, and even those actually living in Luxembourg, consistently resist learning and speaking the most basic Luxembourgish words.

The native Luxembourger is monolingual and will speak only Luxembourgish until education has made him or her trilingual or more.

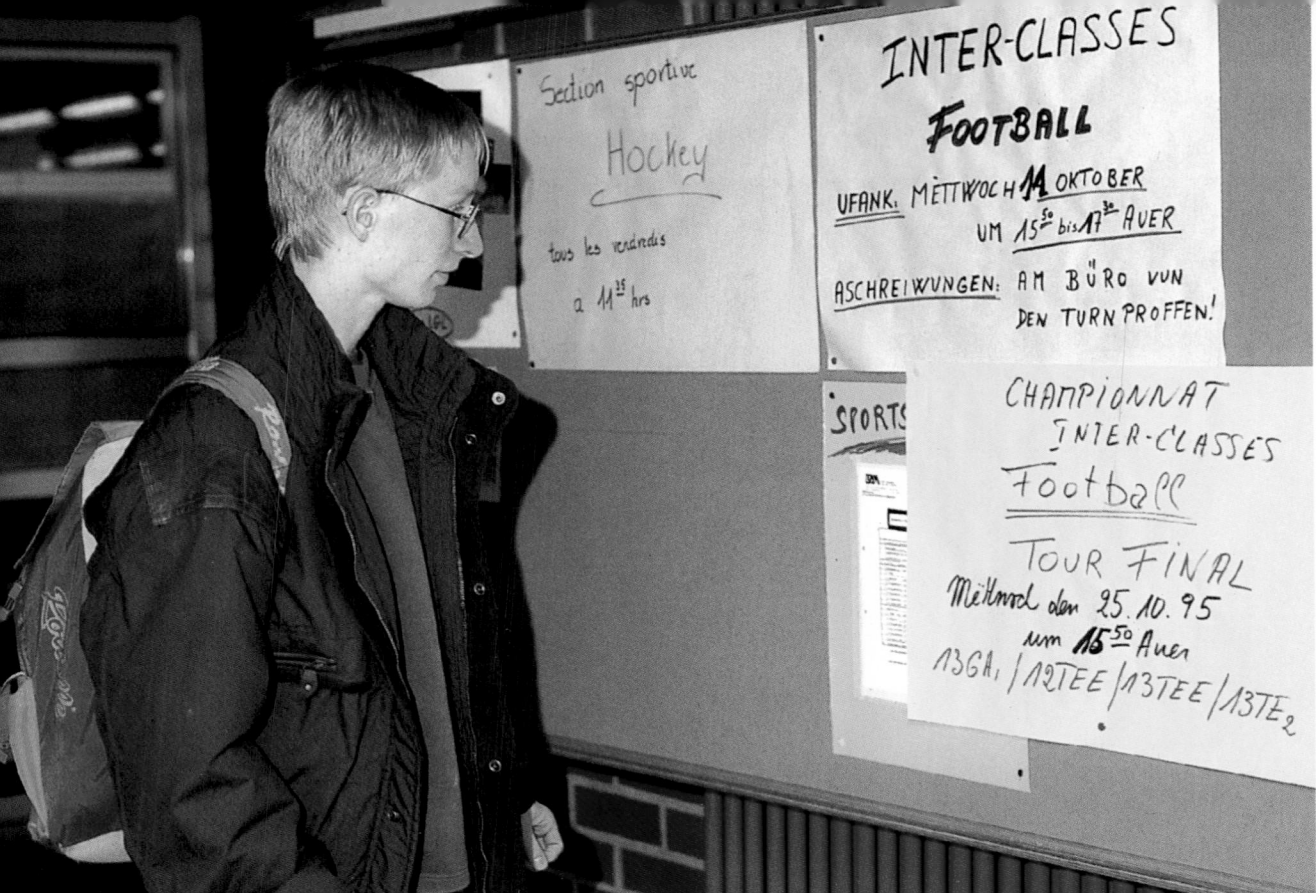

Section sportive

Hockey

tous les vendredis
a 11²⁵ hrs

INTER-CLASSES
FOOTBALL
UFANK: MËTTWOCH **11** OKTOBER
UM 15⁵⁰ bis 17³⁵ AUER

ASCHREIWUNGEN: AM BÜRO VUN
DEN TURN PROFFEN!

SPORTS

CHAMPIONNAT
INTER-CLASSES
Football
TOUR FINAL
Mëttwoch den 25.10.95
um **15**⁵⁰ Auer
13GA / 12TEE / 13TEE / 13TE₂

A student looks at the school bulletin board for the latest sports updates, written in Luxembourgish and French. In primary school, children learn to read and write in German. French is not taught until the second year of primary education.

Luxembourgish was granted the status of a full-scale national language only in 1984. Regardless of that, it has not so far been able to replace the use of German or French in written communication. French is generally used for administrative purposes, while German is used in such other areas as religion and newspapers.

For many people, mastering just their own language can be difficult, yet the citizens of Luxembourg learn three in school. In addition, English is also commonly used. Nevertheless, it is important to realize that Luxembourgers, though justifiably proud of their ability to be gracefully trilingual, are native speakers of neither French nor German.

THREE LANGUAGES, THREE USES

The Luxembourgish language is the language used in everyday life within the family and at every level of society. Spoken by just over 400,000 people in the entire world, it is estimated that 25,000 of these are descendants of the late 19th-century emigrants now living in the United States. All Luxembourgers speak Luxembourgish at home. This no longer implies an association with the working or uneducated classes as it did in the past.

First and second generation immigrants speak the language of their country of origin. In the workplace, Luxembourgers speak Luxembourgish among themselves, but communicate either in French or German with cross-border workers.

In public life, official notices from the government or the administration are drawn up in French, but the use of Luxembourgish is becoming more widespread. The grand duke and the ministers, for example, now always address the nation in Luxembourgish. Justice in the courtroom is dispensed almost exclusively in French, but witnesses may speak in their mother tongues to avoid misrepresenting themselves. For legal contracts, German and French are the only authorized languages. Advertisements are usually bilingual, but the use of Luxembourgish is increasing significantly. Movie theaters generally screen films in their original language, with French and sometimes German subtitles. The Catholic Church uses German in the majority of its written communications, while sermons are spoken more and more often in Luxembourgish. At school, the language of instruction varies with the level of education. Luxembourgish, introduced only in 1912 as an independent subject, is the language of instruction in preschool education from age 4 to 6, as it is in

A class in progress. An educational system based on German until a student is 15 or 16 can prove problematic for immigrant children speaking Latin tongues like Portuguese. As a result there have been moves to introduce French as the principal language from the first year of primary school.

their homes. Luxembourgish is also the language medium in the first two years of elementary school. While German is introduced as the language of instruction during the first year, French enters the curriculum from the beginning of the second. The three national languages—Luxembourgish, German, and French—thus become the basic language subjects at the elementary level. Luxembourg's secondary education offers, in addition to these three national languages, Latin and English.

LUXEMBOURGISH IN THE ARTS

Although a fair amount of classical and modern literature has been written in Luxembourgish, little of it is well known outside the country. Much

---

"AN AMÉRIKA": A POPULAR LUXEMBOURGISH SONG

Michel Lentz (1820–93), one of Luxembourg's most famous national poets, described the sadness of an emigrant who, now in the United States, recalls the charms of his former homeland.

> From my village I came over here,
> which lies deep in the country-green
> over there beyond the big ocean—
> so far from me, so far;
> There stands a poor and tiny house,
> a bench before the door.
> There a lime-tree spreads its leaves
> and gives it a shadowy coolness.
> How deeply aches my heart,
> Give me back my cottage roof.
> I'd give my life's blood for it.

of this work is based on themes common in European literature, then adapted to Luxembourgian life.

Humor and satire are key ingredients. Despite only 400,000 speakers of the language, literary publishing in Luxembourgish is thriving.

Luxembourgish theater is also very popular. All villages or towns with 300 or more inhabitants put on at least one theatrical production a year. An occasional feature film and a number of shorts affirm the viability of a small but superior film industry.

STANDARDIZING LUXEMBOURGISH

An official dictionary was introduced to the population in 1950 after several inconclusive attempts to standardize the spelling of written

A Luxembourger reading in a park while basking in the comfortable morning sunlight. Despite huge strides in the use of Luxembourgish within the country, Luxembourgish is presently not an official language of the European Union, nor is it a working language of the European institutions.

Young immigrants pick up the basics of Luxembourgish in class.

Luxembourgish. Over the years, official government circulars on spelling have been issued, with the last one in 1975. This is a rare example of the success of a legislative measure in imposing regularity upon a previously chaotic linguistic field.

In spite of this, one of the easygoing characteristics of the dialect is the absence of rules and norms, so there is no really uniform language spoken everywhere. An exception to this lack of rules is following the proper way to speak to someone, which is to use the second person singular when the person being addressed is well known or the second person plural when the occasion is more formal or the person is not someone familiar.

LEARNING LUXEMBOURGISH

For such a small country there is a staggering number of local and regional variations of its language. Pronunciation varies greatly even within a few miles. In the south the language sounds like a form of brogue, while in the north there is a clear pronunciation of vowels.

Because the dialect is Germanic, many everyday words are German. Because of the influence of French culture, as many as 1,000 French words are used in everyday discourse as well. For example, the French word for "station," *gare* (GAR), is used, but it is written as *Gare*, since nouns are spelled with capital letters in Luxembourgish, as in German.

There are many "ch" sounds like the one in *loch* in Luxembourgish and "w" is always pronounced as "v." Grammar can vary widely, depending

on where one lives. For instance, the plural of the word "man" is *Männer* (MEN-er) in the south and *Män*, as in "men" in English, in the north.

To greet someone, Luxembourgers say *Moien* (MOY-en) or "hello." If inquiring about a person's health, one would say, *Wéi geet et iech* (Vee geet et eech) or "How are you?" Polite phrases, such as *Wann ech glift* (vun ECH glifft) or "please," and *merci* (mare-SEE) or "thanks," are useful words to know.

POPULAR NAMES

A person with a French first name and a Germanic-sounding surname is likely to be from Luxembourg. Because French has been the official written language for so long, most Luxembourgers tend to have French first names or Luxembourgish equivalents. A common name for a boy, Pierre, will also be expressed as Pier (PE-air). Other typical Christian names for boys are Jhang (ZHUNG)—John in English—and Mätt (MAT)—Matthew in English. Popular names for girls are Marrichen (MA-re-hen) or Mari,

Surnames are usually Germanic, or occasionally Latin, which sometimes was adopted to exhibit the difference between Luxembourg and Germany during the country's Nazi occupation. The most common names are Muller (MULL-er), meaning "miller," Weber (WEB-er), meaning "weaver," Schmit (SCH-mit) meaning "smith," and Schumacher (shoe-MA-her), meaning "shoemaker."

A television crew at work. Luxembourgers have a wide range of channels of different languages to choose from.

and Thérèse (TER-es), Theresa. This custom of French first names is changing with the rapidly growing immigrant population.

BROADCASTING AND NEWSPAPERS

Luxembourg lies at the crossroads of Europe, and residents can easily access French, German, Belgian, and Italian television. Within Luxembourg, there are two giants in the world of audiovisual communications—the RTL Group, which broadcasts over 40 radio and television channels in Luxembourgish, French, German, English, Dutch, and Italian; and Société Européenne des Satellites (SES), which operates the ASTRA satellite system. Radio Luxembourg, a famous station that operated for nearly 60 years with a huge impact on British popular culture, went off the air in 1991.

The RTL Group, which is partly owned by German-based Bertelsmann, has interests in 24 television and 17 radio stations. It also has extensive rights to create catalogs and owns dozens of production companies. The group also provides digital TV and telecommunications and Internet services through its subsidiary, Broadcasting Center Europe (BCE). Digital audio broadcasting, or DAB, has been available in Luxembourg since 2001 when the government amended the legislation allocating frequencies, thus enabling the provision of this service.

WHEN RADIO LUXEMBOURG RULED THE WAVES

When the British Broadcasting Company (BBC) wielded a monopoly over European radio broadcasting in the 1930s, the British public had a very limited choice of programs. Launched in 1933, the Luxembourg station, Radio Luxembourg, built a huge transmitter to reach British audiences. Programs were based on British-recorded dance music and advertisements, made, ironically, in London and then sent over to be broadcast from Luxembourg. It was the first station to give English listeners what they wanted instead of what was thought they should have. A major diplomatic dispute broke out between the BBC and Radio Luxembourg over this, but the station proved to be a huge success and stayed on the air 24 hours a day for almost 60 years, interrupted only by World War II.

Radio Luxembourg was a very international station with German, French, and English services, and even a few weekly broadcasts in Luxembourgish. The English service, broadcast on 208 medium-wave transmissions, came to symbolize nonstop pop music with about 2 million regular British listeners. The first Beatles record ever heard on radio was played on Radio Luxembourg, in 1962—"Love Me Do."

The last words to listeners when Radio Luxembourg went off the air in 1991 were the same that had been used for half a century: "Goodnight, good listening, and good-bye."

One of the more famous Radio Luxembourg disc jockeys was Captain Peter Townsend, who fell in love with a British royal, Princess Margaret, Queen Elizabeth's sister, in 1955. Because he was not a royal himself, and would have had to obtain a divorce in order to marry Margaret, the union was constitutionally barred, which saddened millions of people all over the world. The princess and the captain decided to end their relationship and, sadly, were never to meet again.

SES operates a broadband communications network via the ASTRA satellite system spanning four continents. It currently transmits over 1,000 TV and radio programs and multimedia and Internet services to over 91 million households in Europe.

In addition, environmental groups and groups representing foreigners residing in Luxembourg also have their own radio stations.

The only English language newspaper is the weekly *Luxembourg News*. There are five daily newspapers and, with 358 newspapers circulated per 1,000 people, Luxembourg has one of the highest newspaper readerships in the world. The largest of the dailies, *Luxemburger Wort* (now known as *d'Wort*), publishes in German and French and has a circulation of over 80,000.

The first Luxembourgian publication is believed to be La Clef du Cabinet des Princes de l'Europe, *a Catholic monthly that appeared in 1704.*

ARTS

LUXEMBOURGERS ARE THE BENEFICIARIES of a rich cultural cross-fertilization. The considerable number of immigrants, European Union civil servants living and working in Luxembourg, and the international banking sector, has engendered a flood of national and regional cultural associations from all over Europe. With more than a fifth of the population's being non-Luxembourgers, the country resembles a miniature Europe.

ARCHAEOLOGY

Very few archaeological sites were found in Luxembourg before 1991, when Bastendorf, a Celtic place of worship in the Ardennes, was unearthed. Extensive excavations revealed that the shrine was in use from the first century B.C. until the second half of the third century, when it was abandoned during an invasion.

Situated close to water, which was considered a life-giving element with access to the underworld, the shrine disclosed many offerings of silver coins and jewelry, a common method in that age of expressing gratitude or anxiety. Most notable was the find of curse boards, small lead tablets folded in such a way that the five-line curse would not be visible. Placed in the stream bed of the shrine, these curses would then be fulfilled by the gods of the underworld—it was hoped. It is thought that there were regular gatherings at Bastendorf for religious festivals that included the sacrifice of animals. The specific gods likely to have been worshipped is not clear.

Opposite: **Artistic architectural expression at the DEKA Bank in Kirchberg.**

Below: **The Roman period galleries at the National Art and History Museum.**

95

A display of souvenirs targeted at visitors.

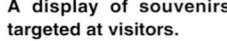

Until the discovery at Vichten, only 4 of the original 46 Roman muse mosaics thought to be in the Low Countries had been found. Archaeologists believe the excellent condition of that mosaic is due to a landslide that covered the area with a layer of clay.

Another very important archaeological discovery was made in 1995 when a farmer from the town of Vichten, in the north, discovered by chance a 72-square yard (60-square m) Roman mosaic on his land. The floor mosaic represents the nine muses who, in Greek mythology, are the daughters of the great god Zeus and Mnemosyne, a titaness representing memory. The muses were thought to inspire music, the arts, and the sciences. The stunning find, dated at A.D. 240, has proved to be one of the largest and best–preserved mosaic works of its kind north of the Alps.

Although other archaeological sites in Luxembourg are minor and comparatively little known, they are, nevertheless, of permanent interest and many have the additional merit of lying off the beaten track. There are Roman baths near the town of Mamer and at four other sites north of the capital city. Another site of interest is the Gallo-Roman complex at Echternach, on the Sûre River, developed between A.D. 50 and 400. What is seen today are the reconstructed lower sections of a 70-room villa, although some of the original stonework is still visible. The extensive Roman remains lie alongside medieval ramparts and an eighth-century abbey founded by the first Anglo-Saxon missionary working on the continent, Saint Willibrord, mentioned earlier.

TRADITIONAL CRAFTS

Most of the traditional crafts have long been abandoned because the Luxembourg market is too small to withstand foreign industrial production. The one remaining craft, pottery making, is itself a very small industry.

A recent development is the production of craft items for home use and decoration that are popular with tourists and are increasingly on display at the various town markets. An example is the *peckvillercher*, a small earthenware bird used as a whistle. Young lovers give them to each other.

THEATER AND CINEMA

The Grand Theater of the City of Luxembourg was built in 1964, with one auditorium seating 1,000 people and another 600 people. During the annual theater season, an international festival of operas, plays, concerts, and ballets with multicultural themes is held. Luxembourg is also a regular stop for many touring theater companies producing various types of plays, including social commentaries.

The town of Wiltz in the Ardennes is the setting for the open-air International Theater Festival in its castle's amphitheater. Each year in July, world-famous actors perform there for audiences from all over Europe.

The Centre National de l'Audiovisuel (CNA) has copies of films made in the last 100 years. The Centre provides a history of filmmaking in Luxembourg and introduces on film four men who played pioneering roles in bringing movies to the grand duchy: René Leclère, Evy Friedrich, Pierre Bertogne, and Phillipe Schneider. The first movie ever made there was shot in 1899, four years after the historic Lumière in Paris projected the world's first public films. An annual film festival shows many new short films that are directed by budding Luxembourg talents.

Luxembourg is the location of an increasing number of production companies. Actions taken by the responsible ministry have resulted in foreign film and television producers transferring some of their activities to Luxembourg. Many European countries want to keep movie and television

The theatergoing audience in Luxembourg is sophisticated in its tastes and appreciates compassionate writing, poetic language, and outstanding acting, regardless of its country of origin.

Edward Steichen (1879–1973), one of the giants of American photography, is held in high regard in his native land of Luxembourg.

screens free of American imports, in gestures to promote European culture, but Luxembourg opposes this and supports increased spending on international media development.

MUSIC

Luxembourg supports a symphony and a chamber orchestra. Concerts are given regularly throughout the year at the Conservatory of Music in the city suburbs. Classical music is very popular with Luxembourgers, with strong support for their chamber orchestra, the European Soloists Luxembourg.

Folk music in Luxembourg is for the most part performed by Guy Schons and his group, Dullemajik (duu-le-MA-jik). At a time when many artists interpret the latest forms of contemporary music to attract their audiences, Schons draws on a repertoire of old classics, rejuvenating them in his own way.

Dullemajik attracts leading singers and musicians, particularly renowned accordionist Maurizio Spiridigliozzi and singer Alexandra Ley.

Although traditional music still commands a following in Luxembourg, the average young music fan is influenced by the international pop charts and the easily available satellite television stations featuring American and English rock and pop performers.

THE EUROPEAN SOLOISTS LUXEMBOURG

The European Soloists Luxembourg is a recent ensemble that unites the best musicians from famous European orchestras in a first-class chamber orchestra, under the direction of the Slovakian violinist and conductor Jack Handler. "Music comes from the heart and is a means of communication," Handler comments.

The orchestra has found a home in the north of Luxembourg, where rehearsals are held. Supported by many patrons, including members of the grand ducal family, it has given many concerts in Luxembourg and in such other European cities as Frankfurt, Budapest, and Paris.

Bagpipe, flute, and guitar players are also in the group, whose fame has crossed national boundaries. The hand-cranked hurdy-gurdy, a stringed instrument heard on the streets of Luxembourg since the 19th century that is used to accompany popular songs and dances, is now played by Schons's musicians.

PAINTING AND SCULPTURE

Unlike many other European countries, the reputation of Luxembourg's artists is not an international one. While there are no great masters from a past age whose achievements can be extolled or whose paintings hang on gallery walls, Luxembourg has produced a number of artists who deserve recognition.

Born in Saint Hubert in the Ardennes, Pierre Redoute (1759–1840) began, at the age of 13, a career that was to make him the most influential botanical artist of all time. In Paris he worked for Emperor Napoleon's wife, Josephine, creating over 600 vellum drawings that are studied to this day.

In the capital city, sculptures can be found around many public buildings.

The main facade of the capital's Municipal Palace, the administrative heart of Luxembourg, bears a unique frieze by Pierre Federspiel. It represents the Countess Ermesinda presenting the charter of freedom to the citizens of Luxembourg in 1244.

Jos Sunnen, who lived from 1894 to 1982, was a classic exponent of the impressionistic style of painting. Frantz Seimetz (1858–1934) painted as a naturalist. Joseph Kutter (1894–1941) was an expressionist painter who introduced modern art to Luxembourg. His most famous painting is "The Clowns." Another famous expressionist painter the country boasts of is Nico Klopp (1894–1930).

The 18th century master sculptors Nicholas Jacques and Jean Georges Scholtus are well known in Luxembourg for their beautiful baroque high altars found in many of the old churches in the Ardennes and Mullerthal areas of the country. The War Memorial, a modern sculpture, is the work of Claus Cito, the victor in an international sculpture competition in 1923.

CULTURAL MONUMENTS AND ARCHITECTURE

In 1994 the World Heritage Committee of UNESCO (United Nations Education, Scientific, and Cultural Organization) placed the old town and fortifications of Luxembourg City on its list of world cultural monuments. Divided into three areas, the first site takes in the ancient quarters, including the original rock the city was founded on. The second area encompasses the governmental quarter, the palace, and the cathedrals. The third contains the battlements and towers that secured the city to the east from the 14th century onward.

Over the centuries, Luxembourg has seen many architectural changes. Many farmhouses from the 16th and 17th centuries still exist, recognizable by their Renaissance-style front doors with coats of arms and partly mullioned windows. The bigger farms often had a large entrance gate to the courtyard. During the 18th century, equally impressive farmhouses were built. Typically, these had symmetrical white facades, window lintels

Many historical buildings in Luxembourg City have been subjected to careful restoration, integrating at the same time some elements of contemporary architecture.

NICO KLOPP

Nico Klopp, the son of a wine grower along the Moselle River, studied at the Royal Prussian Academy of Art in Dusseldorf. There Nico met his future wife and produced his first expressionist woodcuts. Eventually, separated from his wife and daughter, he returned to Luxembourg and survived by selling paintings, preparing illustrations for periodicals, and raising rabbits! Despite living in a small town in the Moselle valley, where artists were not admired, he never gave up painting and engraving. Forced by financial circumstances, he ultimately became a local tax collector.

The first paintings by Nico Klopp were characterized by tragic romanticism. Later works were even more severe, but with a splendid power of light. Often Nico's work met with harsh criticism at home. It prompted debates between art critics who defended classical academic art and others who espoused the avant-garde school of expressionism, as represented by Nico Klopp. Nico himself never took up the battle in the name of his art, although he was a driving force behind the organization of the first "secessionist" exhibition in Luxembourg, in 1927. Significantly, that was 63 years after exhibitions in Paris of Manet and others.

The sole demand of life that Nico made was recognition of his artistic work. For him beauty was the only purpose of art, and he broke away from academic prerequisites and rules, which at that time were the only criteria for the appraisal of art. Sadly, his pursuit of beauty was never understood. Although it meant forgoing financial security, he remained true to his ideal of beauty and of its expression in art. While he achieved a degree of recognition abroad, he was never able to convert this into financial success.

Nico's early death from meningitis, in 1930, at age 36, marked the end of the secessionist period in Luxembourg. The work of Nico Klopp achieved a belated breakthrough only after World War II, with three retrospective exhibitions finally bringing posthumous understanding, appreciation, and respect.

in the shape of segmental arches, and beautifully sculptured oaken front doors framed with stone.

By the 19th century, the most significant buildings being constructed were the manor houses, which retained the symmetrical fronts and stone frames of earlier eras.

MODERN ARCHITECTURE

Modern architecture presents startlingly different concepts, especially office building design, with many of the banking houses and European institution buildings breaking with the tradition that architecture should appear to be classically functional. Some 31 percent of the city center is taken up by offices. In the last decade, however, much of the building growth has taken place outside the center, especially in the Kirchberg Plateau area.

The Court of Justice, a five-story building, was designed by the Luxembourg architect Francis Jamagne and two architects from Belgium. Their vision was to embody "the concept of progressive law in a concrete symbol." The building, erected in 1970 on a raised base in the center of a tiled plaza, with terracing surrounded by native trees, is constructed from a type of steel in which natural corrosion stabilizes after two years, leaving

LUXEMBOURG: EUROPEAN CITY OF CULTURE

A decade after an ambitious cultural plan, the European Cities of Culture, was launched in 1985 through the auspices of the EU, Luxembourg City was chosen to be the European City of Culture 1995. Such a concept of cultural exchange was not a new one for Luxembourg. In the early 1920s, Aline Mayrisch and her husband, industrial philanthropists, welcomed many of the greatest artists, philosophers, and poets of Europe to their home for a dialogue of cultures.

For the organizers of the 1995 festival, the aim was more complex. On one level it was to gather artists of all genres from many countries to present their creations in the grand duchy and thus stimulate artistic production. Another goal, to demonstrate that culture can be an engine of change for positive social growth, reached far beyond that expected of a simple cultural event.

By bringing together local artists with international stars, and by encompassing every field of artistic expression, the desire was to ignite dialogue and to be catalysts for multicultural encounters. Luxembourg is ideally placed, because of its geographical position and mixture of nationalities, to show that coexistence and exchange of different cultures do not lead to the dilution of a country's identity but rather to its enrichment.

The festival, featuring some 500 events, was designed to alternate guest appearances and local productions alongside world premier events. Main productions included a drama by the Chilean writer Marco Antonio de la Parra, the world premier of the opera *Elektra* by Mikis Theodorakis, from Warsaw, concerts by the British Royal and the Israel Philharmonic orchestras, exhibitions of over 250 works by French post-impressionists, as well as original works by Luxembourgian composers, musical performances, and personal encounters with writers, mime artists, and sculptors.

a pleasing bronze surface that improves with age and does not require attention. Another local architect, Pierre Bohler, played a major hand in the design of the European Center, built to host large conferences.

The Hypobank is considered an architectural masterpiece because, inconspicuous at first, the building slowly reveals its true nature with its changing pattern of forms from cubic to cylindrical. An imposing bronze sculpture stands at the entranceway.

Yet another bank, with the entrance hall made completely of glass and a concave grid under a glass roof, is spectacular because of its clear lines, the play of light and shade, and the embrace of the sky as if it were an integral part of the construction.

LEISURE

LUXEMBOURGERS HAVE EARNED a reputation for working hard and taking life seriously. Nonetheless, with an average work week of 39 hours, and at least four weeks of vacation a year, they also have considerable leisure time.

In the 1994 Euro Survey about favorite leisure activities, the most frequent Luxembourgian answers were "sleeping" and "resting." This does not present an accurate picture of Luxembourgers, however. Though they may not be fanatical sports enthusiasts, they do engage in active recreation whenever possible. Fitness and health awareness are concepts that are slowly becoming part of the average person's lifestyle. Still, it would be fair to say that Luxembourgers do like to spend a lot of their free time around the house.

VACATIONS

For many Luxembourgers, vacations are more often spent abroad than at home. With no beaches or mountain resorts in Luxembourg, there is little opportunity for the swimming, sunbathing, or skiing that are to be found in some other parts of Europe.

Moreover, Luxembourg's climate does not really attract Luxembourgers to spend their precious time off in their own country. Warmth and sunshine in the Mediterranean beckon those who can afford it. Reasonably priced package holidays are easily available.

With the opening of the Channel Tunnel, or Chunnel, the great engineering feat under the English Channel linking Europe to Great Britain, Luxembourgers are now increasingly interested in visiting Great Britain.

Above: **Fishing is more than just a pastime for some enthusiasts who take their chances in international fishing competitions that are held from July through October, mostly along the Moselle and Sûre rivers.**

Opposite: **Walking, shopping, and enjoying food and drinks at outdoor bistros along city streets fill many leisure hours.**

In 1995 the
Olympic and
Sports Committee
of Luxembourg
(COSL) organized
the sixth Games
of the Small
European
States, under
the patronage
of Grand Duke
Jean. This unites
the best sportsmen
and women
from European
countries with
populations of fewer
than 1 million
people—Andorra,
Cyprus, Iceland,
Liechtenstein,
Luxembourg,
Malta, Monaco,
and San Marino.
More than
1,000 athletes have
taken part in these
popular Games,
competing in sports
like track and
field, basketball,
cycling, swimming,
judo, tennis,
and volleyball.

NATIONAL SPORTS

Luxembourgers enjoy sports activities, although many prefer to watch rather than to participate. There are 57 sports associations in the country, covering all disciplines. Only a few of these sports, though, are highly regarded or followed avidly by fans.

Luxembourg's true national sport is soccer, which is played at the international level at the European championship matches. Roby Langers was a skilled player and a popular figure in the world of soccer, and one of the few professional athletes native to Luxembourg. Unfortunately, mob violence and hooliganism have marred a number of the European championship games.

American football has never really caught the imagination of Luxembourgers in the same way as soccer, although there is a national team that plays—the Luxembourg Lions. Basketball, with national leagues for women as well as men, is an increasingly popular game and participation in the European championships is taken seriously. Favorite players include the six-foot-tall forward Roby Horsmans and the youthful Marc Schiltz.

The third most popular sport, in terms of the number of spectators it attracts, is tennis. An indoor tennis tournament, the Luxembourg Open, takes place every year. Also growing in spectator attraction is ice hockey, represented by the Luxembourg team named Tornado.

Besides these key sports, there are also many lesser sports in terms of supporters and earning potential, but with more actual participation among Luxembourgers. One is table tennis, exemplified by the skills of Daniel Wintersdorff and Peggy Regenwetter. Another is gymnastics, which is pursued by young people and adults up to championship levels. International semimarathons take place, usually in September, with the course winding through the vine-growing valley of the Moselle.

OLYMPIC CHAMPIONS

Luxembourg's first Olympic gold medalist was Michael Theato (1878–1919), who won the marathon gold at the Olympic Games in Paris in 1900. As no Olympic committee existed in the grand duchy at the time, Theato had to register under the colors of a French club and for a long time was considered to be French. He ran a tactically clever race by letting other competitors lead the event. Coming to the front only at the last 6 miles (10 km), to the applause of 1,500 spectators, he won after 2 hours, 59 minutes, and 45 seconds. He injured himself in his last race, the Tour de Paris, in 1903, finishing in seventeenth place, effectively ending his competitive career.

Joseph Alzin was the second Luxembourger to win an Olympic medal—a silver for weightlifting at the 1920 Games in Antwerp, Belgium. But it was Josy Barthel (1927–1992), winning gold in the 1,500 meters at Helsinki in 1952, who truly won the hearts of the people. Against all odds, Barthel beat the favorite from the United States. In Barthel's words, "I crossed the finish as I had always imagined in my secret dreams: hands up and smiling." Josy Barthel went on to head the Luxembourg Athletics Federation and ultimately the Olympic and Sports Committee of Luxembourg. The main sports stadium in Luxembourg is named after him.

Skier Marc Girardelli, although born in Austria, is now a citizen of Luxembourg and has won the World Cup championship five times. He also carried off two silver medals in the giant slalom and super-G at the Olympic Winter Games at Albertville in 1992. In 1994, at the age of 30, he placed seventh in the World Cup downhill championship race.

The names of Jean-Pierre Ernzen and Nancy Kemp-Arendt, who is also a triathlete, are becoming well known on the marathon circuit.

Swimming has not always been a sport excelled in by Luxembourgers, but that changed with the participation of the formidable Yves Clausse at the Olympic Games in the 1980s and 1990s. Equestrian events, like show jumping and dressage, are also held annually at Cup level.

RECREATION

With a dense network of marked walking paths and special pedestrian circuits through the forests in the Ardennes, hiking is a popular activity

The sport of cycling has many enthusiastic adherents in Luxembourg. The Tour of Luxembourg, a major international bicycle race, is held in mid-June. The last stage is across the hilly Oesling area.

among Luxembourgers. Totally leaving civilization behind is difficult to achieve, though, as one is never more than five miles (8 km) away from a village or farm.

For those who wish to extend hiking excursions into more than day trips, campgrounds are everywhere, and numerous youth hostels are well situated close to campsites should the weather turn rainy. Even in the southern industrial part of the country, walking trails, some up to 73 miles (117 km) long, can be found.

Bicycling is a national pastime. It is not uncommon to see elderly people cycling, too. In the summer the weather is especially inviting for biking through the not-too-difficult Luxembourg terrain. There are traffic-free bicycle trails over much of Luxembourg along the scenic main rivers.

Kayaking and canoeing, as well as other water-related pastimes, are becoming increasingly pursued because of the country's many rivers. Luxembourg also has a number of golf courses. Rock climbing, fishing, and hunting are all popular activities. A particular favorite, especially with young girls, is horseback riding.

ENTERTAINMENT

European Union statisticians, trying to measure the proportion of personal income spent on entertainment in the member states, put the grand duchy at the very bottom of their "EU fun index" in 1994. This low figure of 4.3 percent, however, is not a true reflection of what Luxembourg has to offer.

Nightlife is excellent in Luxembourg, as there is a good mix of bars, restaurants, and clubs run by Luxembourgers as well as other nationalities—one can play darts in British pubs or sing in Japanese karaoke bars. In these well-patronized nightspots, mainstream live music from piano to folk to blues and rock can be found.

International rock-and-roll groups like the Rolling Stones, for example, perform here regularly. The capital is ideally situated to attract crowds of young people from neighboring parts of Germany, France, and Belgium because it is within such easy reach.

Like children everywhere, young Luxembourgers enjoy a day out at a fair.

Other ways Luxembourgers spend their time include watching television, going to movies, and visiting cafés, the equivalent of bars. American and other movies are released early in Luxembourg and are dubbed in French and German. Attending the municipal theater can be difficult, though, as most of the seats are sold-out to season subscribers.

FESTIVALS

LUXEMBOURGERS LOVE TO celebrate festivals and seem to have a fete for almost every occasion, even though the origins of some are so ancient that most people have forgotten what they are.

Many festivals are connected with religious observances, but there are also many that reflect the Luxembourgers' culture and lifestyle.

NATIONAL DAY

Luxembourgers celebrate the birthday of their grand duke on June 23, although his actual birthday is in April. This holiday is also considered the country's National Day. Many Luxembourgers use this day for shopping trips across the border, where it is not a public holiday. All over the country, National Day is an occasion for a happy and festive celebration, with traditional and patriotic processions, religious services, concerts, and public dances.

Festivities start on the day before with members of the grand ducal family being welcomed in various towns and villages of the country. In the evening, Luxembourg City is flooded with lights and a torchlight parade is held, followed by a large fireworks display. On the day itself, crowds gather to watch a military parade. This is followed by a religious service in the cathedral, in the presence of the grand ducal family.

Afterward all the ducal family members make a public appearance on the balcony of the palace. On successive evenings for the rest of the week, various receptions of the diplomatic corps and national notables are held in the palace.

EASTER

On Easter Sunday children traditionally hunt for Easter eggs hidden by the Easter Rabbit, although this is more difficult to carry out in a modern

Opposite: **Local marchers wind down at the conclusion of a street parade commemorating National Day.**

Choosing a *peckvillercher* is fun. Every year, crowds throng the capital city's streets for the Easter market of Émaischen.

apartment than in the Germanic countryside where the custom originated. Once the eggs have all been found, there is a friendly competition among the children, who knock their eggs against each other's eggs. Those whose shells break are the losers. Typically, the four-day Easter holiday is celebrated with the first real spring outing of the year. By this time, the weather will have improved and there is a two-week school vacation.

Easter Monday is a public holiday. In the capital's old town a traditional colorful market called Émaischen (Eh-MAY-schen) takes place. Once, only utilitarian pottery and other household wares were displayed, but now popular arts and crafts are the main items, including the small whistling pottery birds called *peckvillercher*. There are also games for children, folk dances, and singing.

CHRISTMAS

Another two-week school vacation occurs around Christmas, and many families go abroad to escape the cold weather. Stores everywhere during this season are aglitter with decorations, while in the streets everything is festooned and illuminated for the season of happiness and goodwill.

Christmas festivities begin on the feast of Niklosdag (NICK-los-dag), Saint Nicholas Day, on December 6. Each year Kleeschen (CLE-schen), or Father Christmas, dressed in a bishop's vestments and holding a staff, comes down from the skies to reward the children who have been good throughout the year.

He and Housecker (HUSE-eck-er), a black companion dressed in a hooded monk's robe and carrying long sticks with which to chastise naughty children, are welcomed in the various towns and villages. After a procession, Saint Nicholas gives sweets to the children who, until about the age of eight, also get some presents on this day.

Christmas Eve is the family day when children, parents, and grandparents gather around their Christmas tree, listen to carols, and enjoy a sumptuous meal, often of ham or roast pork. Christmas Eve is also one of the few times in the year when children are allowed to stay up later than usual. Frequently, the whole family attends Midnight Mass celebrating the birth of Jesus Christ. Many workers are granted unofficial leave from their jobs for the afternoon.

The lighting of the tall Christmas tree helps get Luxembourg City's residents into a festive mood.

On Christmas Day, a lunch, interrupted only by a televised speech to the nation by the grand duke, is usually hosted by an older member of the family, such as a grandparent. People may be feeling somewhat lethargic after all the eating of the preceding evening. Saint Stephen's Day, Stiefesdag (SHTEEF-fes-dag), the day after Christmas, is another holiday, with yet more feasting.

NEW YEAR

Although New Year's Eve is not a public holiday, employees are usually allowed to go home at noon to prepare for the big night's revels.

New Year's Eve, marking the end of the year, is celebrated more with friends, rather than just family. This can be either at home or in a restaurant. Many of those who eat at home, watching television, will venture out to one of the many "Sylvester" balls, so named because December 31 is Saint Sylvester's Day. These are happy dances in honor of the new year ahead. At midnight everyone wishes each other a happy new year, and people kiss, pop champagne corks, and light fireworks outdoors. The capital city, in particular, gets caught up in the party mood. The atmosphere is one of carnival-style decorations and firecrackers, which add up to a noisy and colorful celebration.

New Year's Day, a public holiday devoted to sleeping late and visiting the family, may seem dull to many Luxembourgers compared with the previous night's excitement, but it is well enjoyed. The prime minister traditionally makes a speech on television as a kickoff to the new year.

CUSTOMS AND RITUALS

January 6 in the Christian calendar is the feast of the Epiphany, marking the day when the three kings (Magi) came to visit the baby Jesus. On this day a special almond cake is baked, containing a miniature figure of a king. In the days of old, the cake contained a simple, plain bean.

A dioramic display depicting the birth of Jesus.

The fortunate person whose piece of cake yields the king's figure—usually one of the children, of course—is appointed king for the day or even a whole week. This lucky youngster enjoys certain privileges, such as the right to decide on the family's meals for the next few days.

Bretzelsonndeg (BRET-zel-son-deg) in March is Pretzel Sunday. Although the sequence of events is the subject of some debate, according to tradition, a young man offers his girlfriend a present on Valentine's Day to proclaim his love. If she responds favorably by offering him a pretzel on Pretzel Sunday, he then confirms his intentions by presenting her with decorated eggs at Easter. Thus Pretzel Sunday has become a day dedicated to lovers and is celebrated by displays of folk art.

On Good Friday, three days before Easter Sunday, a tradition called Klibberegoen (KLI-bare-gurn), or Rattles Round, takes place. According to legend, all the bells in the parish churches fall silent at this time and fly

Luxembourgers enjoy taking part in nighttime processions.

In the town of Vianden in November, Miertchen (MI-air-shen), Saint Martin's Fire, takes place. This ancient custom celebrates the end of the harvest and the payment of the levy to the feudal lord.

away to Rome for confession. To replace the church bells, local boys, and girls nowadays, go around the streets reminding people of Mass by shaking rattles that have a characteristic dry sound.

After the return of the bells to the churches, the youngsters call on each house to collect brightly colored Easter eggs. Other children walk in a procession behind a dog-rose bush, covered in paper flowers and multicolored ribbons, called the Jaudes (YOW-des) or "Judas," for the Judas who betrayed Jesus Christ. After the last Rattles Round has taken place, the Jaudes is burned.

Schueberfouer (SHOO-bare-foor) is celebrated on September 3. Originally a shepherds' market, founded in 1340 by Count John the Blind, it has become the capital's annual giant funfair. It opens when sheep decorated with colorful ribbons are led by shepherds, dressed in folk costume, through the inner quarters of the city. They are accompanied by a band playing a lively tune—the "Hammelsmarsch" (HAMM-els-marsh), the sheep's march. Everyone enjoys the fair's eateries, Ferris wheel, bumper cars, and the friendly bustle.

FAIRS AND FETES

Luxembourg has a long history of fetes and fairs, which are always accompanied by colorful processions, musical bands, flowers, and parades. Every village has its own Kiermes (KEER-mes), or village fair, on the anniversary of the birthday of its local saint.

Carnival week is a week of carefree fun before the somber season of Lent in the Catholic calendar begins, and coincides with a one-week

NATIONAL HOLIDAYS IN LUXEMBOURG

January 1	New Year's Day
March/April	Easter
May 5/6	Labor Day
May/June	Ascension Day
May/June	Whitsun (Pentecost)
June 23	National Day
November 1	All Saints' Day
December 25	Christmas Day
December 26	Saint Stephen's Day (Boxing Day)

school holiday. During this time, the "Carnival Prince" reigns supreme. In 2008, Carnival Week was January 29 to February 4.

In the afternoons there are processions with floats, sessions of public readings, and theme pageants. Costume balls are held in the evenings, with the musicians also in disguise. On Ash Wednesday, which is the beginning of Lent, young people in the Moselle valley carry a huge straw doll through the streets. On a bridge over the Moselle, they set fire to the doll and throw it into the river to herald the end of the joyful carnival.

The first week in May is the beginning of spring fetes, when members of local societies enter the woods to cut the first green branches. These are fashioned into 4-foot (1.2-m) diameter crowns, symbols of the reawakening of nature, called *Meekranz* (MEE-krantz), which are then carried in processions, led by bands in most villages. This is also the time of another public holiday, Labor Day, characterized by trade union rallies with fervent speeches.

Traditional dances such as this provide Luxembourgers with a physical link to their cultural heritage.

RELIGIOUS FESTIVALS

The two-week religious festival of Octave, starting on the third Sunday after Easter, is focused on a pilgrimage, made in honor of Our Lady of

PAGAN PRACTICES

February 2 is Liichtemëss (LICH-ter-mess). This is an end-of-winter ritual devoted to the "new light," or the end of the short, dark days of winter. Children go from house to house carrying candles and lamps and singing traditional songs. Their rewards nowadays are candies, but in olden times, they received more basic necessities, such as lard and peas!

On the 25th day of the same month, Buurgbrennen (BORG-bren-en), or Bonfire Day, takes place. This is another end-of-winter custom from pagan days. Groups of people from various associations such as Boy Scouts, Girl Guides (Girl Scouts), music societies, and fire brigades gather on nearby hills and set fire to giant crosses made of wood and straw. The idea is to expel the darkness of winter. This pagan ritual of burning crosses (which shows the influence of Christianity) forms a chain all over the hills, and is accompanied with barbecues and hot red wine.

A solemn religious procession makes its way through the streets of Luxembourg City.

Luxembourg, to the Cathédrale Notre-Dame in Luxembourg City. Delegations from parishes in all the counties participate in this pilgrimage. Many have to leave home in the night to get there on time, usually traveling on foot as part of the pilgrimage. On the square in front of the cathedral, a fairground atmosphere prevails, with stands selling fried fish, candy, and religious souvenirs. The end of Octave on the fifth Sunday after Easter is marked with a closing ceremony, when stately, solemn processions are held with the royal family and various Catholic dignitaries from abroad taking part in this grand occasion.

Since 1678, Catholics of the grand duchy and neighboring regions have come to the festival to venerate Our Lady, the "Comforter of the Afflicted." The cult of Our Lady remains important to Luxembourg, even in an increasingly lay society, as it also symbolizes national identity and independence. On Ascension Day, another pilgrimage to a nearby shrine dedicated to Our Lady of Fatima takes place.

Whitsun is the name given to the religious time of Pentecost, and it usually falls on the last weekend of May or early June. At the town of Kaundorf, a procession across fields and forests to Saint Pirmin's fountain is held. According to legend, Saint Pirmin was cured of an eye disease at the beginning of the eighth century after rinsing his eyes in the waters of the spring. Healing virtues are still attached to these waters.

Whit Tuesday, although not an official holiday, marks the Echternach dancing procession in honor of Saint Willibrord, who died in Echternach in 739. This unique religious tradition, originally intended as a protection against epilepsy, attracts thousands of pilgrims and spectators.

The dancers, in rows eight or nine wide, traditionally take three steps forward and two steps back. They are joined to each other by white handkerchiefs. Fiddlers who play a haunting polka accompany each group of dancers. This colorful procession winds its way through the old cobbled streets of Echternach before returning to the Basilica church.

Assumption Day, Léiffrawëschdag (LEEF-frow-wusch-dag), is cause for another large celebration in honor of Our Lady. Various herbs, corn, and other plants are gathered into bouquets, which are presented as offerings at various country chapels.

All Saints' Day, which falls on November 1, is a time for religious ceremonies in churchyards. The tombs are blessed, and memories of the dead are revered by family members meeting at the graves of their relatives. The ceremonies are usually followed by gatherings at home or in a restaurant.

The Echternach dancing procession has become one of Luxembourg's biggest tourist attractions, highlighting its colorful cultural heritage.

Whitsun Monday, in May or June, is marked by the broom blossoms fair, Genzefest (GEN-ze-fest), with pageants and flower chariots in the north of the country.

FOOD

THE TASTES OF LUXEMBOURGERS, who are very fond of their food, range widely, because of all the international cuisines represented in the capital. Generally, they like to combine French quality with German quantity. More recently, its food has been inspired by the many historic cuisines of its Italian and Portuguese immigrants.

TRADITIONAL FARE

There are a number of dishes that are considered traditional rural cooking. Such meals are simple and homely in style, but nourishing and wholesome in content.

Typically a first course would be *Bounenschlupp* (BORN-nen-shlup), a bean soup. Many types of beans can be used, but the most common is the broad bean (fava bean). Also eaten as an appetizer are *Quenelles* (keh-nells), small oval-shaped dumplings, stuffed with ground meat or fish. Fish *Quenelles* are prepared with a rich cream sauce, while the meat versions have an equally rich brown sauce.

After the soup or appetizer, a main course follows. Sometimes *Quenelles*, usually meat ones, are eaten as a main meal. Such a dish would be accompanied by sauerkraut and boiled potatoes. One very popular dish is *Judd mat Gaardebounen* (Yudd mat gard-DA-born-nen), smoked neck of pork in a delicious herb sauce, accompanied by broad beans and boiled potatoes. Another is *Träipen* (TRY-pen), black pudding, or small hot sausages, with horseradish, mashed potatoes, and sauerkraut.

Feierstengszalot (fire-STENG-za-lot), a salad composed of sliced cold beef with hard-cooked egg and onions in an oil and vinegar dressing, is a quick and tasty meal. A more acquired taste is *Kuddelfleck* (KU-del-fleck), boiled tripe, which comes from the stomach lining of cattle and is classified as offal. Resembling a honeycomb in appearance, tripe is rich in gelatin, calcium, and iron, with very low caloric value. Tripe usually

Sauerkraut, a German food, is very popular in Luxembourg. Originally devised as a way of keeping vitamin-packed white cabbage through the winter, it is mixed with salt and wine and left to ferment.

Opposite: **The Sunday food market on William Square entices Luxembourg City's food lovers to make choices among hundreds of foodstuffs.**

Shopkeepers put up bright displays to attract customers.

requires prolonged cooking, but it is often sold partly cooked and blanched. *Gras Double Provençal* (grah doobl proh-vahn-SAL), tripe cooked with onion, garlic, and white wine, is a thrifty and flavorful dish.

Delicious Ardennes ham, or *Fierkelsjhelli* (fear-KUL-hel-la), roasted suckling pig covered in an aspic sauce, is reserved for more special occasions. It is usually followed by cheese, particularly *Kachkéis* (KARCH-kays), a typical soft and sticky boiled cheese. Dessert is not normally served with everyday meals, but can be expected to make an appearance at weekend tables, as would liqueurs.

EATING HABITS

A large variety of vegetables, either grown locally or imported from Belgium and the Netherlands, are eaten in Luxembourg. An increasing quantity and diversity of exotic fruit from the Far East and South America can also be found in the markets. Meat, fish, and game are popular, prepared either in a traditional manner or in a slightly more sophisticated style inspired by French cuisine.

122

Most working Luxembourgers take little, if any, food for breakfast, unless they are on holiday and have that extra time. Coffee, rarely tea, bread, and jam is what is usually eaten—a Continental breakfast. Lunch was once the most important meal, but because of working habits and short lunch breaks, the main meal is now taken in the evening between 6:30 and 7:30. One main course is served, with soup as a starter. Cheese is reserved for formal occasions or Sunday meals.

Many workers in the service industries in the capital take their lunch in restaurants, all of which offer varying menus of the day. Great efforts are being made to install cafeterias in schools, which at present close between 12 and 2, when students go home for lunch.

Luxembourgers enjoying the evening at a café in Place Clairefontaine.

Friends enjoying a pleasant meal at a sidewalk restaurant.

A traditional family outing is Sunday lunch or, increasingly, brunch. The meal usually takes the form of a buffet that includes hot dishes. Meals accompanying special occasions, such as anniversaries, success at exams, baptism, first communion, and confirmation, which used to be eaten at home, are now more frequently hosted in restaurants.

SPECIALTIES

Confectionery and assorted chocolates are a special feature in the Luxembourg pastry shops. A true specialty is *Quetschentaart* (ketch-en-TART), an irresistible tart made from small plums and the plum liqueur *Quetsch*.

The best chocolates are those made by hand, using the finest chocolate, fresh cream, and butter, with no added preservatives. Some contain fruit and nuts, while others use liqueur. Somewhat expensive,

In early October, in Vianden, a large walnut market is set up, selling fresh walnuts, walnut cake, walnut candy, and walnut liqueur from roadside stalls.

they are intended for the true connoisseur. Freshly made the day before they are sold, they will not last more than three days, but the difference in taste between these and factory-made ones makes this disadvantage worthwhile.

During carnival season, a special pastry called *Les Pensées Brouillées* (lay PON-say BREW-il-lay), literally "puzzled thoughts," is available in abundance. These are delicious fried knots of dough and are a favorite with young and old alike.

A NATION OF DRINKERS

The range of beers and wines consumed in Luxembourg has dramatically increased and become truly international since the opening of European borders. Special supporting fraternities have even grown up around these two types of drinks. Luxembourg has the highest per capita beer production in the world, but that also includes production for export.

WINE OF MOSELLE

Luxembourg's Moselle region enjoys a very developed wine-growing culture. With temperatures 1 to 2 degrees above the national average and rainfall spread throughout the year, the region provides the ideal climate for producing great character wines.

The Moselle valley, which runs from Schengen to Wasserbillig over 26 miles (42 km) and constitutes the natural border between Luxembourg and Germany, is divided into two parts. The district of Remich, with its heavy and abundant soil, yields a smooth and harmonious wine. In contrast, the district of Grevenmacher is a region with chalky rocks and slow erosion, producing a pure and elegant wine.

As in most of Europe, Luxembourgers prefer their coffee very strong and black. For those with a sweet tooth, sugar is added.

125

Right: **Luxembourgers enjoying local brew in a pub.**

Opposite: **One of Luxembourg's wine caves. The country also has a small, but growing reputation for its liqueurs. *Quetsch*, Mirabelle, Kirsch, and Prunelle liqueurs are all derived from fruit trees.**

Brewing is a traditional industry in the grand duchy, and beer is now produced in modern breweries. "Pure malt and hop" is the motto, and Luxembourg beers, particularly the dark varieties, are becoming increasingly popular abroad.

There is a small family-owned brewery at Bascharage in the south where one can still learn about traditional production processes and can sample its various brews.

WINES

Wines from the Moselle valley have gained a reputation as quality wines for everyday consumption. They are completely different in taste, though not in names, from their German Moselle counterparts. Luxembourg wines are less sweet and resemble those from France.

The "Cremant de Luxembourg" label was introduced in 1988 exclusively for sparkling wines, which are produced by the "method of Champagne." According to this method, after the grapes are pressed, the juice is allowed to ferment in huge metal vats.

The wine is stirred, sugar and yeast are mixed in, and then it is bottled and corked. The extra sugar and yeast cause a second fermentation in the bottle, which makes the wine fizzy. Sediment is removed and then the bottle is recorked. This method is time-consuming and expensive, but results in a very popular export product.

The wine cellars, six in the Moselle valley, are open to visitors in the summer months and are popular spots to visit and do some wine tasting. Some of the smaller cellars have become regular meeting spots for the local older folk on Sunday mornings. In the summer it is also possible to travel the "wine river" on board a cruise ship that plies the Moselle River, calling in at the major towns along the way.

SEASONAL FOODS

From March through the end of September, river fish such as trout, pike, and other highly prized small fish from the Sûre, Moselle, and Our can be found in abundance. Pike is a freshwater game fish that is reputed to kill and eat its own kind. It can grow to as much as 70 pounds (31.8 kg). Those that are usually caught and eaten tend to weigh from 3 to 6 pounds (1.4 to 2.7 kg). The flesh is firm and

During the hunting season, the most common game includes pheasant, young boar, venison, and wild rabbit. The meat is often marinated in red wine and then stewed. Recipes for game dishes are guarded zealously and only the hunters or their wives consider themselves qualified to prepare such meals!

white, but tends to be dry and coarse, with many sharp bones. Though pike can be cooked in a variety of ways, it is most often used to make stuffing for *Quenelles*.

Trout is from the same family as salmon. It has a firm, oily flesh and a sweet, delicate flavor. Trout is a good source of protein and contains small amounts of almost every vitamin. The river trout found in Luxembourg has a skin varying in color from silvery-white to dark gray, and is speckled with red, brown, or black spots. The flesh is white in color. The trout is small, so one fish makes a portion for one person. Trout can be cooked either very simply by grilling, frying, or poaching, or used in *Quenelles*.

EATING OUT

Luxembourg City has a great variety of restaurants, representing all tastes, nationalities, and prices. Restaurant food is popular, as it offers an opportunity for dining out, meeting people, and enjoying food that is too difficult or time-consuming to prepare at home. French fries are frequently ordered, and a selection of vegetables is served with the dishes as integral parts of the meal.

One can choose from Italian or Spanish to Indian, Chinese, or Japanese foods. Pizzerias and Italian cafés are very popular with young people and are often crowded. Also trendy are Spanish restaurants serving tapas (TAH-pahs), snack foods that accompany drinks. Indian restaurants, too, are in vogue.

Within a few blocks, one can find both fast-food chains and Michelin-star restaurants. To savor top-level cuisine at lunchtime, or on Friday and Saturday nights, reserving a table is essential. Competition is fierce, and diners insist on quality and quantity alike. Restaurants can become fashionable overnight and then disappear just as quickly if they cannot keep up the quality or if they raise their prices too much.

People enjoy dining alfresco in Place d'Armes on a spring afternoon in Luxembourg City.

TROUT QUENELLES (*QUENELLES DE TRUITE*)

Quenelles de Truite (keh-nell de TRWEET) is often served as a garnish for any fish dish.

2 tablespoons butter
1/2 cup flour
1/4 cup heavy cream
6 ounces (170 g) trout, skinned, filleted, and ground
1 egg, slightly beaten
1/4 teaspoon salt
1/4 teaspoon white pepper
1/4 teaspoon cayenne

Melt half the butter and stir in the flour to make a smooth paste. Gradually add the cream. Cook, stirring constantly, for about three minutes, until a thick paste forms. Remove from heat and stir in the trout and remaining ingredients. Beat the mixture well, then spoon into a bowl, cover, and chill for 30 minutes.

   With the remaining butter, grease a large saucepan. Fill it half full of water and bring it to a boil. Dip a teaspoon in cold water and scoop out a heaping spoonful of the fish mixture; using another spoon, round off the mixture to make an egg-shaped *Quenelle*. Drop the *Quenelles* into the hot water; cook about eight at a time. Cook for 10 to 15 minutes or until they are puffed up. Using a slotted spoon, remove the *Quenelles* and place on a paper towel to drain off the water. Keep warm until ready to serve. These may be served with parmesan cheese or dill sauce.

CHEESECAKE (*KÈISKUCH*)

For the dough

2 cups flour
1 tablespoon sugar
½ teaspoon salt
2 teaspoons baking powder
½ cup butter, melted
⅔ cup milk

For the filling

1 pound (454 g) ricotta cheese
3 eggs (yolks)
½ cup cream
Juice and rind from ½ lemon
¾ cup sugar
¼ teaspoon salt

After mixing the dry ingredients, add the butter, followed by the milk. Roll out the dough and place in the bottom of a springform pan. Whisk and mix ingredients for the filling and pour mixture on the dough. Bake at 375°F (190°C) for 45 minutes to an hour, until the filling is set. The egg whites may be used separately in another recipe or to make a meringue to be spread on the top of the cake. Whisk the egg whites with some sugar till stiff peaks can be formed with the mixture.

A B C D

1

BELGIUM

Buurgplaatz
(1,834 ft / 559 m)

Clervaux

2

GERMANY

Wiltz

Vianden

Upper Sûre
Natural Park

Kaundorf

Bavigne

Esch-sur-Sûre

Bastendorf

Diekirch

Upper
Sûre

Arsdorf

Ettelbrück

Beaufort

Echternach

3

Oesling

Berg

Vichten

Mullerthal

Redange

Mersch

Noerdange

Eisch

Wecker   Mertert

Grevenmacher

Steinfort

4

Capellen

Strassen

Walferdange

Marner

Wormeldange

Bertrange

Petrusse

LUXEMBOURG CITY

Bettange-sur-Mess

Gutland

Pétange

Bascharage

Alzette

Remich

Rodange

Sanem

Bettembourg

Mondorf-
les-Bains

Differdange

Noertrange

Esch-sur-Alzette

5

Schengen

Dudelange

FRANCE

Capital city
Major town
Mountain peak
Ancient site

Feet   Meters
16,500   5,000
9,900   3,000
6,600   2,000
3,300   1,000
1,650   500
660   200
0   0

N

MAP OF LUXEMBOURG

Alzette River, B5, C4–C5
Ardennes, B1–B2, C1–C2
Arsdorf, B3

Bascharage, B5
Bastendorf, C3
Bavigne, B2
Beaufort, C3
Belgium, A1–A5, B1–B5
Berg, B3
Bertrange, B4
Bettange-sur-Mess, B4
Bettembourg, C5
Buurgplaatz, B1

Capellen, B4
Clervaux, B2

Diekirch, C3
Differdange, B5
Dudelange, C5

Echternach, D3
Eisch River, B3–B4, C3
Esch-sur-Alzette, B5

Esch-sur-Sûre, B2
Ettelbrück, B3

France, A5, B5, C5, D5

Germany, B2, C1–C3, D1–D5
Grevenmacher, D4
Gutland, B4–B5, C4–C5

Kaundorf, B2

Luxembourg City, C4

Marner, B4
Mersch, C3
Mertert, D4
Mondorf-les-Bains, C5
Moselle River, C4–C5, D3–D5
Mullerthal, C3

Noerdange, B3
Noertrange, B5

Oesling, B3
Our River, B1–B2, C1–C2

Pétange, B5
Petrusse River, B4, C4

Redange, B3
Rodange, B5
Remich, D5

Sanem, B5
Schengen, D5
Steinfort, B4
Strassen, C4
Sûre River, C3, D3

Upper Sûre Natural Park, B2
Upper Sûre River, A2–A3, B2–B3

Vianden, C2
Vichten, B3

Walferdange, C4
Wecker, D4
Wiltz, B2
Wormeldange, D4

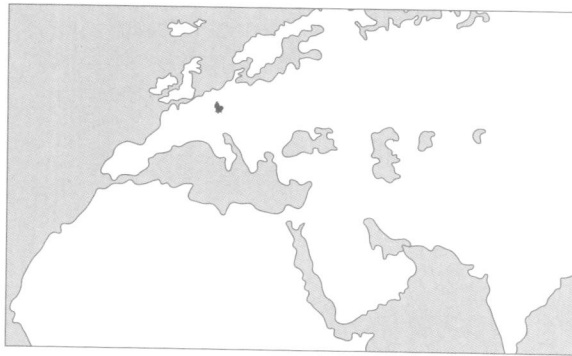

ECONOMIC LUXEMBOURG

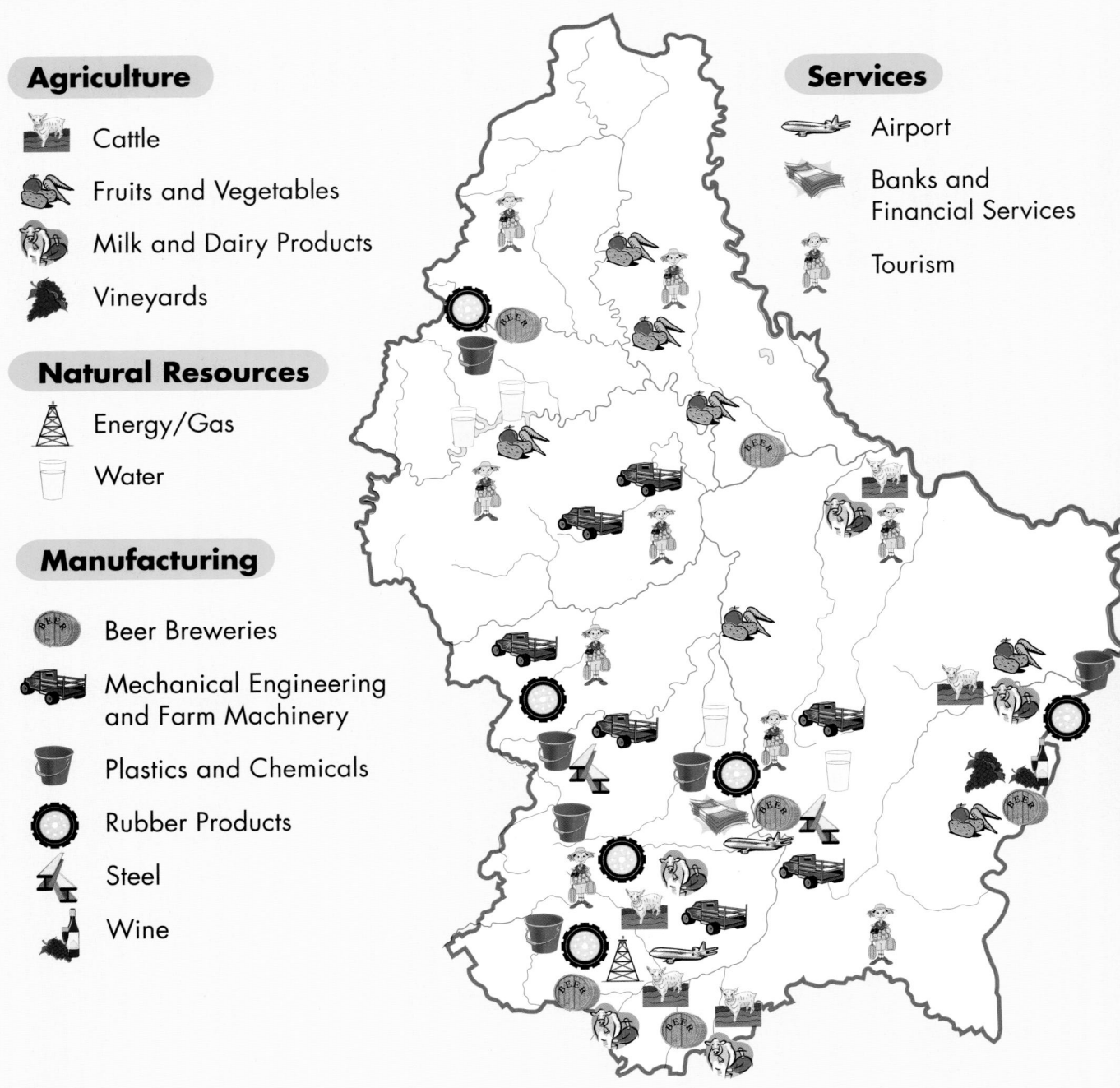

Agriculture

- Cattle
- Fruits and Vegetables
- Milk and Dairy Products
- Vineyards

Natural Resources

- Energy/Gas
- Water

Manufacturing

- Beer Breweries
- Mechanical Engineering and Farm Machinery
- Plastics and Chemicals
- Rubber Products
- Steel
- Wine

Services

- Airport
- Banks and Financial Services
- Tourism

ABOUT THE ECONOMY

OVERVIEW
Luxembourg entered into the Benelux Customs Union in 1948, and joined NATO the following year. In 1957 Luxembourg became one of the six founding countries of the European Economic Community (later the European Union), and in 1999 it adopted the euro currency. Luxembourg has one of the highest standards of living in the world. The country's economy was once based on steel manufacturing. With the decline of that industry, Luxembourg diversified and is now best known for its status as a tax haven and banking center.

LAND AREA
998 square miles (2,585 square km) of which 49 percent is agricultural and 34 percent is wooded.

GROSS DOMESTIC PRODUCT (GDP)
$34 billion (2006 estimate)

GDP GROWTH RATE
6.2 percent (2006 estimate)

INFLATION RATE
2.6 percent (2006 estimate)

CURRENCY
Euro
Notes: 5, 10, 20, 50, 100, 200, 500
Coins (euro cents): 1, 2, 5, 10, 20, 50, 1 euro, 2 euro
USD 1 = 0.74 euro (September 2007)

GDP BY SECTOR
Agriculture 1 percent, industry 13 percent, services 86 percent (2005 estimates)

GDP PER CAPITA
$71,400 (2006 estimate)

WORKFORCE
203,000 (2006 estimate)

UNEMPLOYMENT RATE
4.1 percent (2006 estimate)

NATURAL RESOURCES
Iron ore, timber, quarry stone

AGRICULTURAL PRODUCTS
Barley, oats, potatoes, wheat, fruits, wine grapes, livestock products

INDUSTRIAL PRODUCTS/ACTIVITY
Iron and steel, chemicals, metal products, engineering, tires, glass, aluminum

AIRPORTS
2; Luxembourg-Findel International Airport (with paved runway) and Noertrange Airport (with unpaved runway)

GAS PIPELINE
96 miles (155 km) (2006 estimate)

TELECOMMUNICATIONS
Telephone lines in use: 246,700; mobile phones: 713,800; Internet users: 339,000 (2006 estimates)

CULTURAL LUXEMBOURG

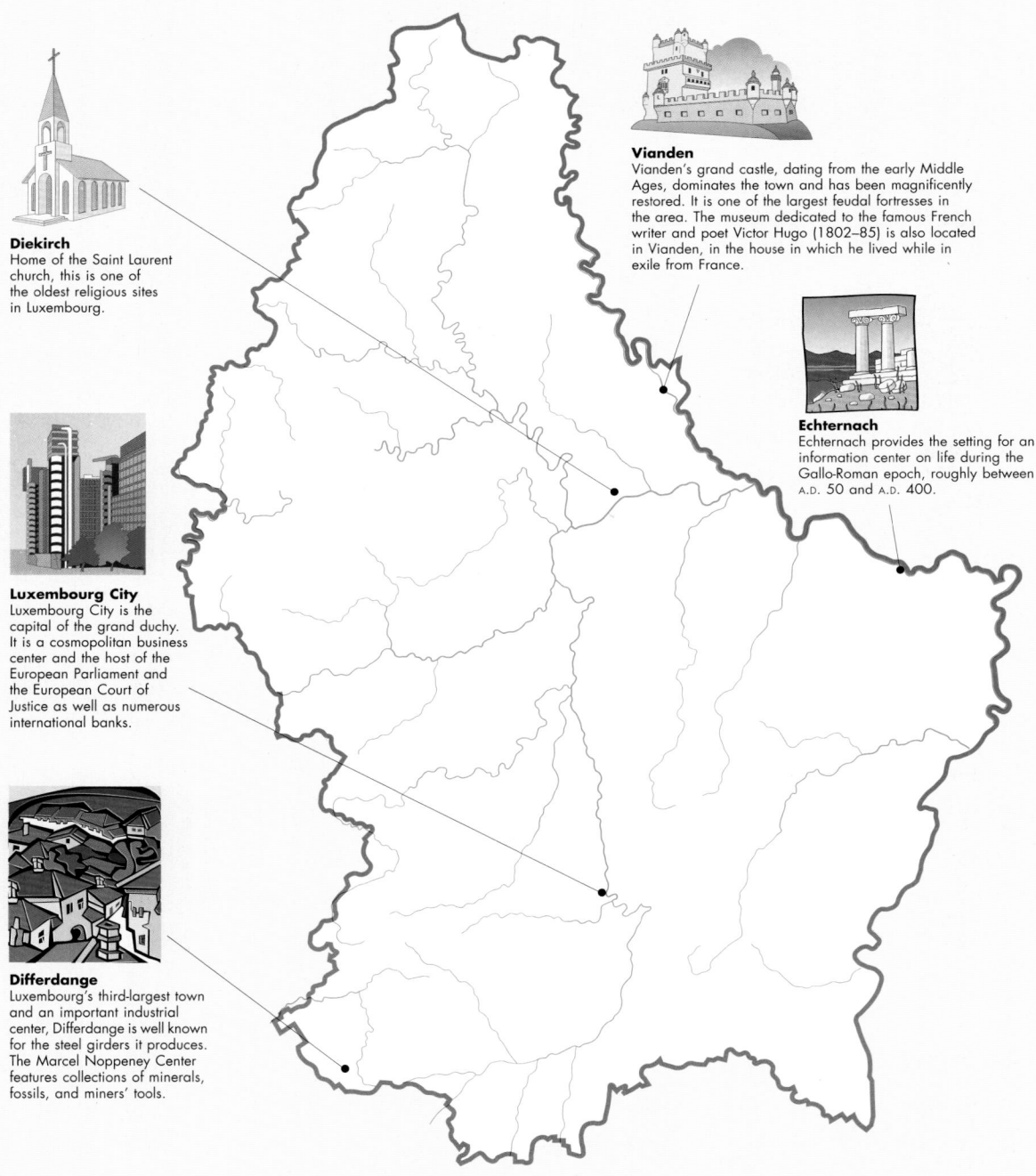

Diekirch
Home of the Saint Laurent church, this is one of the oldest religious sites in Luxembourg.

Vianden
Vianden's grand castle, dating from the early Middle Ages, dominates the town and has been magnificently restored. It is one of the largest feudal fortresses in the area. The museum dedicated to the famous French writer and poet Victor Hugo (1802–85) is also located in Vianden, in the house in which he lived while in exile from France.

Echternach
Echternach provides the setting for an information center on life during the Gallo-Roman epoch, roughly between A.D. 50 and A.D. 400.

Luxembourg City
Luxembourg City is the capital of the grand duchy. It is a cosmopolitan business center and the host of the European Parliament and the European Court of Justice as well as numerous international banks.

Differdange
Luxembourg's third-largest town and an important industrial center, Differdange is well known for the steel girders it produces. The Marcel Noppeney Center features collections of minerals, fossils, and miners' tools.

ABOUT
THE CULTURE

OFFICIAL NAME
Grand Duchy of Luxembourg

POLITICAL STATUS
Constitutional monarchy under a system of parliamentary democracy

FLAG
Rectangular panel with three horizontal stripes of red, white, and blue (from top to bottom)

COAT OF ARMS
The coats of arms of the Grand Duchy of Luxembourg are on three scales: small, medium, and large. They were established around 1235 by Count Henry V of Luxembourg. The coats of arms are essentially composed of 10 alternating stripes of silver and blue, with a clawed red lion on its hind feet over all, crowned with gold, its tail forked and looped. From 1123, Count William of Luxembourg wore a striped banner on his equestrian seal. The majority of the descendants of the first House of Luxembourg used horizontal bars, while the coat of arms of the House of Namur featured a lion. The coats of arms have enjoyed legal protection since 1972.

CAPITAL
Luxembourg City

POPULATION
480,300 (2007 estimate)

POPULATION GROWTH RATE
1.207 percent per annum (2007 estimate)

BIRTHRATE
11.9 births per 1,000 Luxembourgers (2007 estimate)

AGE STRUCTURE
0-14 years: 18.8 percent (male 46,478/female 43,656)
15-64 years: 67 percent (male 161,466/female 158,261)
65 years and over: 15 percent (male 28,530/female 41,831) (2007 estimates)

DEATH RATE
8.42 deaths per 1,000 Luxembourgers (2007 estimate)

LIFE EXPECTANCY
Total average: 79.03 years; male: 76 years; female: 83 years (2007 estimates)

ETHNIC GROUPS
Native population is ethnically German and French. Immigrants, accounting for 37 percent of the population, include Belgians, Italians, Portuguese, and others from the Balkan states of Bosnia and Herzegovina, Montenegro, and Serbia.

RELIGIONS
Roman Catholicism, Protestantism, Orthodox Christianity, Judaism, and Islam

LANGUAGES
Luxembourgish, French, German

TIME LINE

IN LUXEMBOURG	IN THE WORLD
	753 B.C. Rome is founded.
	116–17 B.C. The Roman Empire reaches its greatest extent, under Emperor Trajan (98–17).
	A.D. 600 Height of the Mayan civilization
	1776 U.S. Declaration of Independence
	1789–99 The French Revolution
	1869 The Suez Canal is opened.
1921 The grand duchy signs the Belgian-Luxembourgian economic union (UEBL).	**1914** World War I begins.
1940–45 Luxembourg is again invaded by German forces. The grand duchess and the government go into exile. Battle of the Bulge. General George S. Patton liberates the nation.	**1939** World War II begins.
1944 Signature of a draft agreement of a customs union between Belgium, Luxembourg, and the Netherlands (Benelux).	**1945** The United States drops atomic bombs on Hiroshima and Nagasaki.
1949 Luxembourg is one of the founding members of newly created NATO.	**1949** The North Atlantic Treaty Organization (NATO) is formed.
1951 Luxembourg is one of the founding members of the European Community of Coal and Steel (ECCS), the forerunner of the European Union (EU).	
1952 Luxembourg City is chosen as the provisional headquarters of the ECCS.	

IN LUXEMBOURG	IN THE WORLD

1957
Ratification of the Treaty of Rome, which creates the European Economic Community (EEC) as well as the European Atomic Energy Community (Euratom). The treaty is signed by the Benelux countries and Italy, Germany, and France.

1966–69
The Chinese Cultural Revolution

1986
Nuclear power disaster at Chernobyl in Ukraine

1991
Breakup of the Soviet Union

1997
Hong Kong is returned to China.

1999
The euro is adopted as the official currency in 11 countries of the European Union, including Luxembourg.

2000
Crown Prince Henri becomes grand duke of Luxembourg on the abdication of his father, Jean.

2001
Terrorists crash planes in New York, Washington, D.C., and Pennsylvania.

2003
War in Iraq begins.

2004
Prime Minister Jean-Claude Junker is again invited to form a government after his party wins the general election.

July 2005
Voters back a proposed EU constitution that had been rejected earlier in the year by French and Dutch voters.

GLOSSARY

Bounenschlupp (BOHN-nen-shlup)
Bean soup, most commonly broad bean (fava bean), to start off a meal.

Bretzelsonndeg (BRET-zel-son-deg)
Pretzel Sunday.

Burgbrennen (BURG-bren-en)
Bonfire Day, an end-of-winter custom performed in February.

Émaischen (Eh-MAY-schen)
Traditional market held on Easter Monday in Luxembourg City.

Fierkelsjhelli (fear-KUL-hel-la)
Roasted suckling pig covered in an aspic sauce.

Gras Double Provençal (grah doobl proh-vahn-SAL)
Tripe cooked with onion, garlic, and white wine—an economical Luxembourgian favorite.

Hammelsmarsch (HAMM-els-marsh)
The sheep's march, a lively tune played during the shepherds' market.

Housecker (HUSE-eck-er)
Father Christmas's black companion, who carries a long stick to chastise naughty children.

Jaudes (YOW-des)
A dog rose bush covered in paper flowers and multicolored ribbons, made for the Rattles Round.

Judd mat Gaardebounen (Yudd mat gard-DUH-born-nen)
Smoked neck of pork in herb sauce, with broad beans and boiled potatoes.

Kachkéis (KARCH-kays)
Soft and sticky boiled cheese.

Kiermes (KEER-mes)
Village fair held on the anniversary of the local saint.

Kleeschen (CLE-schen)
Father Christmas.

Klibberegoen (KLI-bare-gurn)
Rattles Round, where children go through the streets, using rattles to remind people of Mass in the three days leading up to Easter Sunday.

Kuddelfleck (KU-del-fleck)
Boiled tripe.

Liichteméss (LICH-ter-mess)
End-of-winter ritual celebrated in February, when children carry candles and lamps and sing traditional songs.

Miertchen (MI-air-shen)
Saint Martin's Fire, an ancient custom in Vianden to celebrate the end of the harvest with huge bonfires and a torchlight procession.

Quenelles (keh-nells)
Small oval-shaped meat or fish dumplings, which can be either an appetizer or a main course.

Schueberfouer (SHOO-bare-foor)
Former shepherds' market, now a giant amusement park in the capital.

Stiefesdag (SHTEEF-fes-dag)
Saint Stephen's Day, the day after Christmas, which is also called Boxing Day.

FURTHER INFORMATION

BOOKS

Needham, Ed. *Belgium, Luxembourg, and the Netherlands (Focus on Europe)*. Mankato, MN: Stargazer Books, 2004.

Press, Petra. *European Union (World Organizations)*. Milwaukee, WI: World Almanac Library, 2003.

Simons, Rae. *Luxembourg (The European Union: Political, Social, and Economic Cooperation)*. Broomall, PA: Mason Crest, 2005.

Smith, David Andrew. *George S. Patton: A Biography*. Westport, CT: Greenwood Press, 2003.

WEB SITES

EarthTrends: The Environmental Information Portal. http://earthtrends.wri.org/text/

Europa. The EU at a Glance. http://europa.eu/abc/index_en.htm

European Commission. http://ec.europa.eu/

French-at-a-touch Travel Guide. http://www.french-at-a-touch.com/Countries/Luxembourg/luxembourg.htm

Le gouvernement du Grand Duché de Luxembourg. www.gouvernement.lu/

Luxembourg Presidency Publications. www.eu2005.lu/en/savoir_lux/lux_publications/

Portals to the World. www.loc.gov/rr/international/european/luxembourg/resources/lu-geography.html

STATEC Economic and Social Portrait of Luxembourg. www.portrait.public.lu/en/introduction/index.html

U.S. Department of State on Luxembourg. www.state.gov/r/pa/ei/bgn/3182.htm

MOVIE

Congé fir e Mord' (Vacation for Murder)—first feature film ever made in Luxembourg in the Luxembourgish language (1983).

BIBLIOGRAPHY

Barzini, Luigi. *The Europeans*. New York: Simon and Schuster, 1983.
Cameron, Fiona. *We Live in Belgium and Luxembourg*. Sussex, England: Wayland, 1986.
Lewis, Flora. *Europe*. New York: Simon and Schuster, 1987.
Stevenson, Victor. *Evolution of Western Languages*. New York: Van Nostrand Reinhold, 1990.
Central Intelligence Agency—The World Factbook. www.cia.gov/library/publications/the-world-factbook/geos/lu.html

INDEX

agriculture, 9, 44–46, 50, 52, 65
archaeology, 95–96
architecture, 100–103
Ardennes, 7, 95, 97, 99, 100, 107, 122
army, 25
arts, 95–103

banking, 44, 37, 38, 40, 41, 43, 95, 102
Belgium, 7, 10, 19, 21, 38, 47, 39, 79, 102, 109, 107, 122
Benelux countries, 7, 25
Benelux Customs Union, the, 25
biodiversity, 52–53

birthrate, 57, 71, 82
Bonaparte, Napoleon, 22
businesses, 15

Caesar, Julius, 19
casemates, 14, 23
Celtic and Roman rule, 19
Celts, the, 19, 47
Chamber of Deputies, 29, 9, 30, 31, 34
cities, 14–17
    Esch-sur-Alzette, 15, 8
    Luxembourg City, 7, 21, 32, 35, 66, 77, 100, 103, 113, 118, 111, 118, 128, 129

citizens, 26, 29, 58, 63, 80, 86, 99
cliffs, 14
climate, 12–13
coat of arms of Luxembourg, 33
confectionery and chocolates, 124–125
conservation, 8
constitution, the, 29, 30
constitutional monarchy, 29
constitutional rights, 29
    freedom of opinion, 29
    freedom of the press, 29
    freedom of worship, 29
Council of Ministers, 27
Court of Auditors, the, 41
craft products, 42

crime, 73–74
customs and traditions, 115–116

dams, 11
drinking water, 11, 75
drunk driving, 74
dukes, 19

economy, 37–47
education, 29, 30, 68, 70, 71, 70–71, 82, 86, 87, 88, 85
elections, 29, 13, 30, 34, 35
electoral districts, 30
electricity, 31, 47, 65
Émaischen, 112
Emperor Augustus, 19
employment, 8, 38, 47, 38, 50
energy, 44, 39
entertainment, 109
environment, 49–55
    1965 Nature Protection Act, 54
    air pollution, 8, 44, 37, 42, 46, 116
    conservation measures, 54–55
    environmental politics, 49
    Green Alternative Party, the, 49
    greenhouse gas emissions, 49–50, 44
    Kyoto Protocol, 49, 41
    Ministry of Environment, 50
    waste management, 51–52
    Water and Forest Administration, 54
    water pollution, 49
environmental consciousness, 75
equality, 9
Ermesinda, 29
EU Environment Council, 49
euro, 27
Europe, 20, 125
European Coal and Steel Community (ECSC), 25
European Court of Justice, 26
European Economic Community (EEC), 41
European Investment Bank, 27
European Parliament, 44
European Union (EU), 26–27
exports, 47

fairs and fetes, 116–117
family, 67
fauna, 8
festivals, 111–119
    Christmas, 112–114
    Easter, 17, 13, 111, 112, 115, 116, 117, 118, 117
    New Year's Day, 114–115
films, 37, 10, 54
financial and commercial sectors, 89
financial services, 43–44
flora, 8
food, 121–131
    eating habits, 122–124
    traditional dishes, 121–122
forests, 7
France, 7, 126
French Revolution, 22

game hunting, 53
geography, 7–17
Germanic Confederation, 22
Germanic Franks, 19
Germany, 7, 27, 29–35, 29, 31, 62, 65, 85, 91, 109, 125
global recession, 43
government, 24, 22, 24, 22, 32, 49, 71, 73, 87, 90, 92
Grand Duchess Charlotte, 24
grand duchy, 19, 37, 42, 43, 44, 63, 65, 79, 85, 97, 103, 109, 107, 118, 126
gross domestic product (GDP), 37, 71
Gutland, 8, 54

history, 19–27
holidays, 117
    National Day, 11, 111, 117
hydroelectric power, 33, 47

imports, 47, 98
independence, 21, 23, 22, 63, 118
industrialization, 44, 57, 20
industries, 17, 26, 75, 39, 40, 68, 123
infrastructure, 8, 19, 43
insurance, 38, 44, 72, 73
Internet, 69, 92, 93
investment, 33, 43, 40

Iron Age, 19, 37
iron and steel works, 9
Italy, 25

jurisdiction, 32
    Constitutional Court, 32
    courts, 32
    minister of justice, 32, 35
    police, 32, 35, 73, 74

landscape, 7, 46
language, 85–93
    French, 15, 21, 23, 22, 57, 58, 59, 63, 86, 87, 91, 85, 86, 87, 88, 90, 91, 92, 93, 103, 109, 107, 121, 122, 128
    German, 24, 21, 25, 50, 59, 61, 86, 87, 91, 85, 86, 87, 88, 90, 92, 93, 109, 121, 126, 121
    Luxembourgish, 85, 86, 87, 88, 89, 90, 91, 92, 93
laws, 27, 29, 30, 32, 37, 43, 44, 51, 68
legislation, 30
leisure, 105–109
Lentz, Michel, 33
life expectancy, 71
literature, 88
Luxembourg Model, 39
Luxembourgian presidency of the EU, 49

Maastricht Treaty, 26
machinery, 41, 42, 47, 80
manufacturing, 38, 39, 41
maps
    cultural Luxembourg, 136
    economic Luxembourg, 134
    map of Luxembourg, 132
marriages, 26, 20, 21, 67
media and communications, 39
medical care, 72–73
medieval castles, 10
medieval times, 20–21
Mediterranean, the, 46, 105
Middle Ages, 42, 78
minerals, 9
    iron ore, 9
minimum wage, 39

mountains, 7
multilingual cultural events, 15
museums, 47, 82
    Natural History Museum, 55
music, 98–99

names, 91–92
national anthem, 33
national flag, 33
natural habitats, 54
Netherlands, the, 7, 122
newspapers, 92–93
nongovernmental organizations (NGOs), 54
North Atlantic Treaty Organization (NATO), 24, 19, 21, 22
nuclear weapons, 34

Oesling region, 8, 9
offices, 15, 31, 102
Olympic champions, 107
Organization for Economic Cooperation and Development (OECD), 24

painting and sculpture, 99–100
parks, 8, 65, 72
Patton, General George, 25
pensions, 40, 34, 19, 26
places of worship, 82–83
    Cathédrale Notre-Dame, 77, 15, 60, 118
political parties, 30
    Christian Social Party (CSP), 34
    Democratic Party (DP), 34
    Green Alternative Party (GAP), 34
    Luxembourg Socialist Workers' Party (LSWP), 34
population, 14, 62, 95
poverty, 39
prices, 39, 128, 129
prime minister, 27, 115
public debt, 37

radio, 33, 92, 93
rainfall, 8, 12, 125
recipes
    cheesecake, 131
    trout quenelles, 130

recreation, 77–83
religion, 77
    Christianity, 78–79, 77, 78, 79, 81
        Protestantism, 15
        Roman Catholicism, 21, 14, 20, 45, 79, 10, 109
    Jesuit Order, the, 7
restaurants, 34, 19, 123, 124, 128, 129
Rhode Island, 10, 21
rivers, 10, 54, 101, 81, 82, 83, 79
    Alzette, 10
    Eisch, 9
    Moselle, 10, 82
    Our, 10, 66, 127
    Pétrusse, 10
    Rhine, 8
    Sûre, 8, 96
Roman Empire, 19
royal family, the, 32–33
ruins, 66

school holidays, 82
shopping, 33, 71, 23, 105, 111
social security, 34, 27
social services, 73
Spain, 21, 8, 10, 79, 80
sports, 8, 86, 105, 106, 107, 106
    canoeing, 11, 108
    kayaking, 11
    sailing, 11
state education, 29

taxation, 37, 43
television, 92–93
temperatures, 12, 125
textiles, 47
theater and cinema, 97–98
topography, 7
tourism, 8
towns
    Belvaux, 17
    Differdange, 17
    Dudelange, 9
    Echternach, 11, 26, 96, 119
    Esch-sur-Sûre, 16, 15
    Rumelange, 26
trade, 8, 44, 37, 49, 52, 65, 117
trade fairs, 42–43

traditional crafts, 96–97
transportation, 22
treaties of Utrecht and Rastadt, 22
Treaty of London, 22
Treaty of the Pyrenees, 22

unemployment, 37, 38, 61, 72
United Nations (UN), 24, 49, 55, 62, 67, 100
United States, 37, 8, 55, 59, 60, 73, 72, 73, 74, 87, 88, 107
Upper Sûre Lake, 8
Upper Sûre Natural Park, 8
urbanization, 15, 52, 54, 53

valleys, 7, 9, 13, 14, 46, 54
vehicles, 43, 50
villages, 9, 47, 67, 89, 111, 113, 117
vineyards, 9, 10, 11, 46

wars
    Battle of the Bulge, 25, 78
    Spanish Civil War, 22
    World War I, 24, 37
    World War II, 7, 24, 23, 26, 33, 34, 60, 62, 63, 83, 93, 101
welfare, 71–73
Western Europe, 9, 22, 68
William I, 22
William II, 24
William III, 22
wineries, 9
wines, 10, 35, 62, 125, 126, 125
witchcraft, 80–81
women, 35, 80, 106

youths, 69